Does the thought of sending to school for the first time panic?

Are you afraid to send your child to a public school?

Do memories of your early school years still haunt you?

Would you like some pointers on how to start your son off on the right foot?

If the answer to any or all of the above is "yes," then you've come to the right source. In *The First Three Years of School: A Survivor's Guide,* Dr. Cliff Schimmels draws upon his experience as an educator and a parent to offer you comforting, specific suggestions you can follow to help your son or daughter adjust to the schooling process. With his positive insight, enlightening observations, and compassionate point of view, Dr. Schimmels enables you to understand more of what your child will experience and clarifies your role in helping him do his best. He helps you see what these years mean in the whole period of his development. As your child starts school, you know that he's not the only one who has many adjustments to make. *The First Three Years of School: A Survivor's Guide* will give your son or daughter and you more confidence about these critical years.

BY Cliff Schimmels
How to Help Your Child Survive & Thrive in Public School
How to Survive & Thrive in College
When Junior Highs Invade Your Home
The First Three Years of School: A Survivor's Guide

Cliff Schimmels

The First Three Years of School

A Survivor's Guide

Fleming H. Revell Company
Old Tappan, New Jersey

Library of Congress Cataloging in Publication Data

Schimmels, Cliff.
    The first three years of school.

    1. Child rearing. 2. Home and school.
3. Education, Primary—Curricula. 4. Parent
and child. I. Title. II. Title: First 3 years
of school.
HQ769.S287   1985   649′.124   84-11668
ISBN 0-8007-5175-2

TO Mary

Writing about child rearing is at best a presumptuous task; but I have a valuable source of help—a wise wife—one who is charming enough to encourage me, diplomatic enough to allow me to make some mistakes with her children, and unselfish enough to let me participate in some of the success and claim some of the ideas.

It seems rather paradoxical that I dedicate this book to her. Not only did she type it, proofread it, and supervise the writing, but she lived through and demonstrated the suggestions not once but three times.

In humble ways, I express my gratitude for all of this, and so much more.

Contents

The First Three Years of School

1

With a Six-Year-Old and Panic Time

Okay, so you have a brand-new six-year-old—and you are about to panic. This is what you have been waiting for for years—the time when he (or she) gets out of diapers, learns to feed himself, carry on a conversation, and wander a little farther out of the nest into that strange world outside the home.

This is supposed to be a happy time: a time when you can breathe a bit, fix your nails, wash the car, take some walks alone—when you can trust yourself to be away from that precious child for a few hours a day.

And in the face of all these pleasant possibilities, you are about to panic. One moment you look at your child, remembering all your investment of time and love, and he looks so grown-up, so mature, so independent, so ready to face about anything. Then the next minute you look back to see if your first appraisal was accurate, and you see a fragile infant with his innocence and emotions hanging from the end of his nose just waiting for some outsider to chip away at all that you have grown to love in your child.

In search of some comfort in this dilemma—or at least some understanding—you are driven to the books and magazine articles by all the popular experts on the subject of child rearing; and now you are even more confused. Each one says something different; and each says it so persuasively you feel that if you don't agree, you should be ashamed of yourself. Frankly, I don't know what is harder, trying to rear a child or trying to sort through all the books on the subject.

Here is this one author telling you that anyone who sends a six-year-old to school is an insensitive beast, and the other person tells you that to keep a child home from school will cheat him out of all his social opportunity and charm. One person tells you that Christians should send their children only to Christian schools if they expect anything good to happen; but another one says that public schools aren't all that bad.

So here you are, trying to be the best parent you can in the midst of all that diverse and often confusing advice. I don't blame you. I think I would panic too. I am just glad that my three are past that stage so now I can speak as an expert on the subject.

Don't get me wrong. I am not trying to make light of your problem. Those are tough decisions, but you are basically in the battle all by yourself. For one thing, you are the one who is going to have to live with the child long after you have made that decision. You are the one who is going to have to live with the eventual outcome. (Scary, isn't it?) Besides, you are the only person who knows your child well enough to make the decision about what kind of school is best for him. Sure, you can get a lot of advice from a whole pack of outsiders, but any decision you make regarding anything about your child, especially his education, should be tailored to his specific needs, feelings, and abilities. No one else knows your child well enough to make that kind of decision. Read and listen to the advice, but always measure it against what is best for that specific and very special creation.

Now, let's suppose that you have decided to send your child to school—Christian or public. You have considered all the evidence and all the alternatives, and you have decided what is best for you, for the family, and for the child. You are convinced, or at least you are prepared to live with the decision.

Now what? Good question! You are definitely not finished. You know that. You didn't need me to remind you. During the next three years, your child is going to need intelligent parents and a supportive family more than at any other time in his life, except when he is very young and totally dependent. It is very important for you to understand your child during this time, for you to understand what he is going through, for you to understand what is happening to him at school so you can complement and supplement all of his outside activities and bring them together to form a well-adjusted child.

That is the purpose of this book—to help you gain some understanding about what is happening to your child in that strange world of school, so you can encourage him, support him, and fill in the gaps the outside agencies miss. In the meantime, I would also like the book to be encouraging. Being a parent is a frightening and often consuming task, but a lot of people are succeeding. In fact, that is the one thing we *can* learn from reading the books on child rearing—there are a lot of good parents at work. And anyone who is concerned enough about his child to worry about the decisions he makes has a head start in the direction of being a good parent. I commend you for your interest.

Although the book covers a wide range of suggestions and ideas about dealing with the child in those early years of school, all thoughts are centered around five common themes. Perhaps if you can get a grasp of these before you start reading, you will be able to make more practical use of the suggestions as you find them. Again, I am not necessarily interested in persuading you of the authority of the themes, but I offer them as a reminder and (I hope) as encouragement.

1. I have chosen to focus this book on the child's growth in the first, second, and third grades, or what are commonly known as the primary years.   This focus may come as a bit of a shock to you, depending on where you live. With the heavy emphasis on nursery schools, preschools, prekindergartens, toddlers' campuses, and kindergartens in some areas of the nation, you may get the idea that your child is almost halfway through his formal schooling career by the time he gets into the first grade. Why do I insist on using this as the place of beginning?

Well, I chose this span of school for several reasons. For one thing, those early-childhood education programs (anything below first grade) vary so much from community to community and state to state that it would be difficult to get an accurate view of what might be happening in your specific community.

In some places, the educational opportunities (schools) for three-, four-, and five-year-olds are almost as structured and demanding as the programs for first, second, and third graders. In the communities where these programs are so highly developed, there is usually a concentrated push to get the children involved, at least before they enter kindergarten. The promoters of these programs would have you believe that if your child doesn't participate, he is going to be educationally "behind" for the rest of his life.

On the other hand, in a few states, some children don't even have an opportunity to go to a standard kindergarten, much less to a prekindergarten, a pre-prekindergarten, a pre-pre-prekindergarten, or to a prenatal academy. They have to make do with the traditional routine of starting school at six.

In some of these preschool programs, the students and the teachers get right down to the serious business of learning with studies in readiness, colors, numbers, alphabets, and so on. Others are more like group baby-sitting services with a story thrown in once in a while as a means of keeping the children quiet. Both provide socialization opportunities, of course, but the educational demands do vary.

Since there is so much variety in both the expectations and

structure of these early-childhood programs, I have chosen to concentrate on the first grade as a beginning point just so I can acknowledge some uniformity. Regardless of the "pre-programs," all communities recognize a standard first-grade experience.

If your child has already been involved in one of these structured, preprimary educational opportunities, you will find some of the suggestions and analyses in this book applicable to your child at an earlier age, so you will just need to readjust the information down a year or two. On the other hand, some of the topics in this book are directly related to first, second, and third grades, regardless of what earlier experiences your child has had. The timing of some lessons and some adjustments is a matter of age and maturity and not a matter of training or instruction.

While I am on that subject, let me add that, as an educator, I think of those prekindergarten programs as available services. If your circumstances make such programs valuable to you, you should avail yourself of these services. If your child needs a little bigger environment to learn to play, if he shows an unusual aptitude for reading activities, or if you need to be away from your child a few hours a day, it is good for you to have the opportunity to send your child to a nursery school.

But from an educational point of view, the structured school experience at that age isn't completely necessary. If your child doesn't need such an experience, or doesn't have the aptitude for it, and if you are a conscientious parent who uses good language around your child and reads to him regularly, he is not going to lose all that much educationally by staying home with you.

Now, I realize that last statement opens the gate for a whole avalanche of controversy, but I am confident in my position. In fact, I have just recently verified it in school settings.

First, I asked several kindergarten teachers. Some assured me that they could usually tell which children had been in previous programs. Next, I went to the junior high school and asked eighth-grade teachers. They had no idea which children had started to school early; and when I asked them to guess based on students' educational abilities and maturity, they were wrong as often as they were right.

I do not question the quality or value of early-childhood programs. If you and your child are ready and need such services, I thank God that they are available. But because of the variety in such programs, I have chosen to focus on first, second, and third grades to represent the beginning of the school experience.

2. *I believe that the span between ages six and eight constitutes one of the most critical periods in human development.* Sure, I have to say that. Everyone who writes a book or gives a speech about a particular age group has to make some kind of statement claiming it to be the "most critical age." But in my case, it is more than an attention getter. I am serious.

Someone once said, "Give me a child until he is six and he will be mine for the rest of his life." I am not really sure who said it. I have heard it attributed to every subversive group known to man. But who said it isn't important. What is important is the truth in the statement. Those early years are significant. During those first three years in school your child will encounter more new things than he will during any other three-year period of his life. Of course, every three-year period of development is important for one reason or another. The period between ages eight and eleven is a time of solidity. The period between eleven and fourteen is a time of adjustment and change. The period between fourteen and seventeen is for trial and error. The period between seventeen and twenty is a time for transition from authority to self-identity.

But during those years between six and eight, your child will establish a base of brand-new skills and attitudes that will serve him the rest of his life. It is imperative for all of us, parents and teachers, to cooperate in helping him get that base right. It is this imperative that gives this book its purpose.

Of course, each of the three years is different. First grade is a time of beginning. During his first-grade year, your child will be introduced to more new experiences than during any other year in his life. And among those new experiences is that awesome, mysterious experience of learning to unravel the mysteries of the universe and the Creator through the printed word. Simply stated, he will learn to read.

The thrill of newness carries a particular challenge to the learner and to the family who shares that thrill with him.

Second grade is a time of mastery. The child has learned to read, to count, to write, to sit still; he has learned to learn. Now, during second grade he will have to grow with his newfound skills. He will have to master them. This time the thrill will not be in the newness, but in the freedom that comes from being able to do things on his own.

Third grade is a time of transition. The child has learned and mastered new skills. Now, he must perfect those skills so that he can say good-bye to a child's world and begin to enter a world of independence and increased responsibility. When he learned to write in first grade, he learned to print. That's child's writing. In third grade he will put aside that child's writing and write like an adult in cursive.

In fact, writing serves as a symbol of the whole third-grade experience. Here the thrill is in the anticipation. The child can see a bigger world of independence ahead of him.

Again, although each of the three years is a different experience, the package constitutes a crucial age. If any one of these years doesn't go right, the child will probably have some extra work in the future to compensate. During this period, the child needs his family, but he needs a family that understands his increasing need for freedom and independence.

3. *I am not afraid of schools.* Now, I know that I may be in danger of losing my credibility with that claim. You may even accuse me of not being able to read, since it seems as if the only thing the newspapers can print is how our schools are failing us. Well, I have read those charges, but I still make the claim. Before you write me off as a political activist, a nineteenth-century idealist, or an ostrich with his head stuck firmly in the sand, let me state my reasons.

First, I visit schools. I am in schools more than 100 days a year. Given the fact that your child is only in school about 180 days, I am there almost as much as a student. During the past three months, I have been in forty-three different school buildings in four states. I have visited more than 200 different classrooms.

Guess what I found? I found warm, caring teachers who were working hard at providing every one of their students a maximum learning experience. Oh, I found some bad ones, too. I won't lie to you. But I found a lot of good ones; enough to give me confidence in what schools are doing. Every parent needs to understand that caring teachers and loving parents have the same objective—to get the child through childhood and adolescence and into adulthood as a sensitive, intelligent human being committed to doing what he can to serve God. Although some teachers are better at it than others, most are nevertheless trying. For that reason, I have confidence in schools.

Next, I believe in schools because I have confidence in children. I believe in a child's ability to sort through, discern, forgive, and forget, when forgetting is called for. In other words, I believe in a child's resilience.

I have come to this belief from both teaching and parenting experiences. When I was a young teacher I made a lot of mistakes. At times, I was downright stupid, and maybe even cruel. I still wake up in the middle of the night, thinking about some of those blunders. For protection, I now try to avoid those towns where I spread my youthful incompetence. I don't want to go back and remind myself of how bad I was. I would prefer that those people never think of me. There is no need to remind them. But, I can't escape. Some former student finds out where I have been hiding all these years. He calls me and invites himself and his family to come and remember old times. I shudder; I live in dread; I try to rationalize my youthful errors. I think about leaving town without a forwarding address. But the day comes; the student arrives; and we have a great time. Never once does he even hint that he remembers all those stupid incompetences I plagued him with. If he does remember, at least he has not let those incidents bother him to the point of destroying him. Could it be that his youthful resilience has blocked them out of his mind?

I see the same thing in my own children. Now that they are edging toward adulthood, they seem to have forgotten all the stupid things I did to them when they were younger. Or at least, if they haven't forgotten, they don't tell on me in front of my friends or my mother.

Sure, I know children get hurt. They are hurt by insensitive teachers, insensitive students, and insensitive parents; and they are hurt by their own childish play. Of course, my first impulse is to want to keep them from those hurts, to build a wall around them, and protect them from all suffering. But we can't do that— not realistically. Hurting is a part of life, so what we must do is to help our children encounter and endure the hurts that come. Now, I don't advocate beating on them once a week just so they will get used to it, but I do think children can handle the normal hurts that come through a social situation, such as the school or home, if we will help them.

Another reason I believe in schools is that regardless of how much time a student spends in school or thinking about school, the school is never more than the second most significant influence in his life. And that leads me to my fourth theme.

4. The home is the most significant, most influential child-rearing and educating institution in this country.   I realize this is my common theme, but I am going to say it again and often. Regardless of where you decide to send your child to school, regardless of how much money you spend on his education, regardless of how good or bad his teachers are, you are still the most significant influence in his development. If he is going to learn to read, count, add, multiply, tie his shoes, tell time, find his way home, drive, write poetry, play baseball, love, care, or worship, *you* are going to have to teach him. Oh, you can expect a little help from some other places such as the school or the church. But you may not get it; and at best, it is only help. If your child is to become educated, *you* have to assume the responsibility. After all, he is your child.

I warn you. This theme comes through in this book. If you are looking for ways to make those other agencies do your work, you have come to the wrong place. I am interested in offering suggestions that will help you do your job as a parent.

5. I believe in childhood.   I believe that every person is entitled to a childhood—a time relatively free of restrictions and unrealistic demands and undue expectations. In fact, I think that most people are going to have such a time. If they don't have a childhood when they are young, they may have one when they get a little older. Knowing this, it always seems to make sense to let a child be a child during childhood so he won't feel cheated when he gets to be an adolescent.

So, if you are looking for suggestions about how to turn a child into an adult in some overnight operation, you won't find them in this book. I believe in such things as play and snowballs, and play acting, and pet frogs, and learning to count, and innocence, and embarrassing questions. If you are looking for a superkid or a baseball star or a musical virtuoso, you may have to read another book.

The theme here suggests that we respect childhood as a time as free from pressures and unnecessary anxieties as we can make it. There is a whole lifetime for such things.

As parents, your job now is to help your child get through those first three years of school with a solid enough base in learning skills, self-identity, and fear of God that he can grow toward becoming what God has created him to be.

To begin that job, let's look at the school to see what help you can expect from that institution.

NOTE: In order to save space throughout this book, I will refer to your child with the pronouns *him* or *his*. If this isn't accurate, please substitute the appropriate word, and forgive me. I have a short stubby pinky, so I have trouble hitting that slash key anyway.

Also, I will refer to primary teachers as women. I realize that there are some excellent male first-, second-, and third-grade teachers, and I don't want to cast anybody into specific vocational roles. But since more than 90 percent of the primary teachers are women, I have chosen the common term for the sake of brevity.

Chapter 1 at a Glance

1. With the increase of Christian school opportunities and home-school opportunities, parents now have the privilege and responsibility of making significant decisions concerning their children's education.
2. Know your child. Know what he needs educationally.

3. Study the school you choose for your child. Make sure it provides the educational opportunities your child needs.

4. Early-childhood educational programs (preschool, nursery school, prekindergarten) are available services. Use them if you and your child can profit from them.

5. The primary grades (first, second, and third) are important years because your child is making the adjustment from homelife into school life. You need to be close to him during those years so you can understand and supplement.

6. Childhood is not a disease to be cured as rapidly as possible. Christ recognized it as a special time. Although you want your child to get started right, you want to make sure he enjoys the opportunities of childhood.

2

School Notes

To too many parents, the school is an austere, alien monster that snatches up our children at nine o'clock every morning and spits them back to us at three-thirty every afternoon. I am not sure who is responsible for this Chasm of Misunderstanding that separates schools and parents, but it is unfortunate. As you start your child on that twelve-year trek called school, you need to know something about the whole institution so you won't feel you are sending your child off to a foreign country each morning. For an elementary review, I offer the following personal observations about American education.

1. Schools and parents have the same objective. As your child starts school, this is the first point you need to understand. The school really has the same goal as you—to get your child through childhood and adolescence and into adulthood as a responsible, thinking, sensitive, moral, educated human. If you have any arguments with the school, those arguments are usually about methods and techniques—about means but rarely about goals.

If you will accept this point, you will be in a better position to help your child coordinate the two major influences in his life—family and school.

2. The teacher is the key to the whole educational system. Regardless of what the laws say, regardless of how the building looks, regardless of the quality of the textbook, the classroom teacher is the key to educational quality and direction. As far as your child is concerned, that teacher *is* the educational system. If she is sensitive and committed to the task of teaching, your child will find that the American educational system is in fairly good shape. On the other hand if the teacher is rude, incapable, or too tired to teach anymore, your child will find that American education is in a sorry state.

I realize that this is an oversimplification of all the political and social powers and issues at work in our schools, but there are no laws nor administrative decisions that require teachers to be incompetent, insensitive, rude, arrogant, worldly, domineering, noncreative, dull, or intolerant of the child's convictions. If the teacher displays any of these characteristics, she chooses to do so.

If you are sincerely interested in helping your child make the most of his first three years in school, you will direct your attention to that individual classroom teacher. Throughout the book, I will make specific suggestions about why and how you can establish a working, healthy, productive relationship with the teacher.

At this point, you may be tearing at your hair and shrieking about my naiveté. You may even accuse me of being an idealist. You have been around teachers before; and you are convinced that they are too self-sufficient, too arrogant, too complacent to be interested in talking to parents. Let me assure you. That is only a front. Teachers are as frightened of parents as parents are frightened of teachers. Do your child a favor. Break down that barrier. Help your child's teacher be a success with at least one student.

This may not be as difficult as it sounds. From my general observations, I find that some of the best teachers in the nation are assigned to the primary grades. In fact, many districts will assign only experienced, proven teachers to first grade. You just may find that the teacher, the key to educational quality, is your most capable helper in this task of rearing your child.

3. American education is a ladder system that permits students to climb up one rung at a time. As the student completes the primary grades (first, second, and third), he moves to upper elementary (fourth, fifth, and sometimes sixth.) From there, he goes on to junior high or middle school and then to high school.

4. Although we Americans appear to have a love affair with test scores, we really don't make any significant decisions based on those scores. In some countries, all children are tested at about the end of the upper elementary level. If the child's scores are high enough, he gets to go on to high school which prepares him for college. But if his scores are too low, he goes immediately into a vocational school which prepares him for a blue-collar career.

We could get into a lively debate about the pros and cons of both systems, but what this means to your child is that if he falls behind academically during his early years in school, he still has a chance to catch up later. In other countries, the children do not always have that opportunity, so many of them encounter more academic stress than do most American children.

I offer this observation to help you filter through some of the information that suggests schools in other countries do a better job of education. Often they do a better job simply because the situation applies more pressure to the student to succeed.

5. The American educational system was designed to be a local operation. The founders of this country originally intended for the local communities to raise the money and make the decisions for their educational system. Thus, we have local districts, local school boards, and local property taxes. But in the interest of achieving some kind of uniformity and consistency, states established laws and agencies to make sure the local communities were doing their jobs well. So now we have state laws regulating such things as certification of teachers, building safety, attendance policies, graduation requirements, selection of textbooks (in some cases), and school buses.

In recent years, the federal government has entered the scene, particularly with laws regarding the full rights of citizenship to all people regardless of race, sex, or ability. Now, the federal courts have been assigned the primary responsibilities of making sure the local districts comply with federal laws.

I offer this information in case you want to protest a policy or practice. In order to be effective, you will need to know who made the decision. Let me illustrate. Most states have a law that allows the school bus to pick up only those children who live farther than one and a half miles from school. If your first grader has to walk a mile, you may want to complain to the principal. But don't be surprised if you get nothing but sympathy. He is only following a state law.

6. In most districts, teachers are now organized through membership in one of two organizations—National Education Association (NEA) or American Federation of Teachers (AFT). Thus, a strike is always a possibility. Without getting into all the political ramifications and issues, let me say only that a strike does interfere with education, and this interference could be particularly costly for a child in the first, second, or third grade. I am not interested in telling you how you should feel about striking teachers. That is your business. But I do want to convince you that you need to be prepared to help your child deal with a teachers' strike. I hope some of the suggestions in the book can provide direction if you need it.

7. School years and school days are fairly uniform across the nation. Almost every state works on the basis of a 180-day school year, but this may fluctuate by as much as 5 days depending on how the state counts teacher conferences. In most schools, the primary day is between five and five and a half hours.

You may be interested in following some of the current discussion about lengthening both the school day and the school year. In several states, there is presently a general feeling that more is better.

8. *In most primary classes, there are too many students.* This is a little piece of judgment that ought to send some school administrators' blood pressures up a notch or two. But I am convinced. This past year I visited several primary classrooms. I visited one school that had classes of twelve, fourteen, and seventeen students. I visited other schools with as many as thirty-two students in one class. Regardless of how good the teacher is, the educational experience in a second-grade class of fourteen is a qualitatively different matter than the educational experience in a class of thirty.

The reason I make this point so emphatically here is that so much of the learning during the primary years is personal learning, requiring attention and drill. Throughout this book, I suggest ways for you to supplement your child's schoolwork. In the midst of all these suggestions, you may throw up your hands and yell, "If I have to do all this, what's the teacher supposed to be doing?" But as you give your child five minutes of personal attention on some drill such as multiplication tables, think about how long it would take a teacher to give thirty students five minutes of personal attention.

After having been around schools for forty years, I am convinced that if we want to do something to improve the quality of educational experience for our children, we will begin to focus our efforts on lowering the class size. But how do we do that? We hire more teachers, and that means more taxes. Where is our priority?

9. The special educational programs are the best they have ever been, and they are still improving. Schools have come into some bad publicity recently. Some people have even suggested that they used to be better than they are now. But one area of marked improvement is in the field of special education and services, which includes about 20 percent of our children. We now have both the laws and the facilities to help most children who have special learning needs. If your child has a problem, either minor or major, the school is committed to providing him with appropriate help. If you suspect your child has some special problem that is preventing him from learning at the maximum of his potential, check with the teacher. She will know how to have the child tested, and she will know where to get the help.

Although reading these nine observations won't tell you all you need to know about schools, it should help you realize that school is not a foreign country. It is simply an institution designed to support you in that awesome task of rearing your child. If you and the school can know each other well enough to cooperate on that assignment, together you should be able to provide a healthy climate for your child as he goes through this period of rapid growth and change.

Chapter 2 at a Glance

1. To provide the best situation for the child's growth, the home and the school must come together on such matters as objectives and procedures. To achieve this, you need to know what the school expects. Ask!
2. Visit the school often so that you won't feel it is an alien world.

3. Since the classroom teacher is the key to the whole educational experience, get to know this person.
4. Politically, the school (both private and public) is a grass-roots institution. Individual parents do have a voice in policies and procedures. To make your voice effective, study the mechanism of the institution.
5. As your child is gaining basic learning skills during his first three years in school, he will need supervision while he practices. You will need to provide some of this supervision.

3

The Growth Marks Scattered
Around the House

Last summer, we painted the living room. In other words, Mary painted and I offered daily critiques. One of the most difficult parts of the job was deciding what to do with that special door sill. You know the one—the door sill where each year for the last ten years we lined the kid up on his birthday, put a straight edge across his head, and recorded his height with a bold pencil mark.

To an outsider, those pencil marks might have looked like just another smudge; but to us, children and parents, they were significant. They recorded growth—the progress in each child's drive toward becoming an adult. And those smudgy marks did more than just record changes in physical growth. They were also symbols of changes in attitude, awareness, capability, and independence. Oh, there was a lot of memories wiped away with one stroke of a paint brush.

Since that age between six and eight is so full of growth and memories, both for the child and for the parent, these special marks merit some consideration. Let's ask four questions: What are these growth marks the child is likely to encounter? What is the value of achieving these marks? When is the child likely to achieve these marks? How can the parents help him achieve and remember?

What Are the Growth Marks Your Child Is Likely to Encounter During His First Three Years in School?

Sometimes an adolescent or even an adult backs out of some task or new experience by saying, "I have never done anything like this before." Now, imagine how many times a courageous child between the ages of six and eight will do something he has never done before. In these three years, your child is going to master for the first time a whole bundle of skills that will become lifetime tools. His growth can be observed and recorded as he moves through these physical, intellectual, and social accomplishments. Just to get an idea, let's make a list of some of the things you can expect your primary child to do for the first time in his life.

- Ride a bicycle
- Tie his shoes
- Dress himself
- Use his own housekey
- Tie a necktie
- Write his name
- Count past ten (or one hundred)
- Read a book
- Sleep over at a friend's house
- Spend most of a day away from home
- Tell time
- Bake a cake
- Complete a needlepoint project
- Make his bed
- Pull a tooth
- Get a new tooth
- Read
- Multiply
- Write cursive
- Understand fractions
- Write a story
- Go on a field trip

Although you may want to protest some of the items on the list because your child has already mastered that particular growth mark, or because he may not be ready for a specific mark until he is past the age suggested, at least consider the reason for my making the list. In the next three years, your child is going to achieve a number of one-time accomplishments; and these accomplishments need to be recorded, remembered, and perfected.

What Is the Value of Achieving These Marks?

Obviously, there are skills on this list which are vital to the child's functioning as a student and as a person. If he does not master the skill at an appropriate time or he does not master it with a certain degree of proficiency, his whole growth schedule will suffer.

Beyond that, mastering these growth marks has an even greater value. These are accomplishments, major accomplishments, which have the same psychological value as any other of life's accomplishments. They provide the child with a means for understanding himself.

As achievements, these growth marks contribute to the child's building a healthy respect for himself. When he accomplishes some task such as tying his shoe, he suddenly realizes that he is important and capable. He feels good. He has achieved something and he knows it. He is making progress in this journey through life. Being able to do the task is reward in itself. You may catch him practicing over and over. In fact, he may make a nuisance of himself, bothering you for any opportunity to perform his newly acquired growth mark.

This is all quite healthy, and you should help him celebrate. For one thing, performing the task is encouragement within itself. The child is building a self-image by doing something on his own.

In this case, he doesn't have to depend on someone else's praise. He can see that he is accomplishing something.

Let me illustrate. If you ever saw me, you would say I lie; but I have run a marathon. No fooling—26 miles, 385 yards, and a couple of extra inches thrown in for good measure. Now, I could have played church league softball for a hundred years and listened to all those supporters yell such things as, "Nice hustle," "Way to go," "Good hit," "Way to throw," and "Nice try even though you made an out," but all that together wouldn't have done nearly as much good as the day I staggered across that finish line of the marathon. I didn't need praise. I didn't need to spend any time wondering if your words were sincere or just empty vessels trying to cheer me up. At that moment, I was aware of what I was capable of doing with what God had given me. I was aware that, as a creation of God, I probably had more potential than I will ever realize. And in this context, the event gave me purpose and dedication.

Now, to a sophisticated adult, tying a shoe may not seem like a very big deal. But to a child, the event could have the same psychological effect that my finishing the marathon had. Achieving that small event could help him realize that as a child of God, he is a capable human being, and this realization will help him develop a positive self-image, and that self-image will enable him to continue to grow and learn.

When Is the Child Likely to Achieve These Growth Marks?

Timing natural growth is always a tricky business. The other day, I asked the expert down the street when I should pick my apples. He said, "When they are ripe." I was never so embarrassed in my life, until I realized that I say the same thing to parents.

If I have done a good job of convincing you of the importance of those growth marks in your child's development during his first three years in school, you may want to ask, "When should I expect him to achieve these?" And I would answer, "When he is ready."

I offer this profound advice with one purpose. I don't want you to panic. I just can't stand to see mothers and fathers cry or grandmothers lose bragging rights in a crowd. But sometimes the adults in a child's environment put too much emphasis on *when* the child masters these one-time accomplishments.

I have listened to these games. "Jerry used the potty when he was three months." "Sally swam at one year." "Pete is just three years old and he is already riding a motorbike." By the time I get into the conversation, I can't think of anything colossal enough to get anyone's attention. What is the parent of a typical child to do?

Let's start this discussion with an obvious but often forgotten point. Intelligence or native ability is one thing, but maturity is something else. Not all children mature at the same time. Some children are ready for new experiences earlier than others. Some children master hand and eye coordination a little earlier. Some children are ready for certain growth marks earlier than others. You know that. It is just hard to remember sometimes.

Just because one child is a little earlier in developing than another doesn't mean that he is brighter or more gifted or more intelligent or has smarter parents or nicer grandmothers. It just means he is maturing a little quicker at this stage of his development. If your child is a little slower, it isn't anything to be ashamed of. Just stay out of those conversations that make you feel guilty. On the other hand, if your child is one of the quicker ones, enjoy it. He may not always be the earliest maturing child on the block or in the family. Child development is a little fickle that way. The natural development in childhood is not always scheduled to accommodate parents' wishes or expectations.

If you had a child who didn't lose his first tooth until he was eight, you probably wouldn't hold it against him. You might take him to the dentist just to check, but once you were assured that everything was in its natural order, you would probably forget all about it and just wait until the child's mouth finally decided to cooperate. Why can't we be that understanding with a task such as reading or counting to 100?

Despite how this might sound to you, I am not really trying to minimize the importance of teaching or expectations or even progress. I don't propose a freewheeling approach that advocates letting the child run wild in the streets. But at the same time, I do suggest that we recognize the child's right to develop on the schedule God has ordained for that particular child. I propose that we don't panic just because the child develops a little more slowly in some area than some other child. I propose that there is a difference between maturity and ability; and that we shouldn't confuse the two.

If I could convince you of this one point, first-, second-, and third-grade teachers all over the world would nominate me for the Nobel Peace Prize. The unfortunate custom that puts all children in the first grade at six years of age sometimes makes a mockery out of the Creator's genius in making each of us special. Most are probably ready for the experience and can progress rather well. But some children simply aren't mature enough physically to handle the mechanics of first-grade learning. Personally, in retrospect, I think I must have run into a problem here. I am right-handed. I do only one thing with my left hand. I write, and I write upside down the way normal left-handers do. So why does a normal right-hander write with his left hand? It is probably because of some maturity problem. I probably wasn't mature enough physically to hold the pencil properly when I started to write, so I worked out a compensation method. As far as I know, I have suffered no permanent damage from the malady. When I was younger, I took a lot of verbal abuse from teachers and fellow students about the messiness, but I lived past that.

The point is that I probably wasn't mature enough to do first-grade work when I was six. It wasn't a matter of intelligence. I probably wasn't physically able to do what the other children were doing. Apparently, my problem wasn't severe enough to cause any great stir; but if it had been, what would have been the harm for me to have delayed first grade another year. When one puts his life into a fifty- or seventy-year perspective, starting school at six or seven is not really that big a deal. As parents, we must make decisions not for the moment and not for the month, but for a whole life span. And to make intelligent decisions, we must recognize each child's special maturity schedule.

Now that I have convinced you of that point, let me say something that may sound almost contradictory. When it comes to timing the growth marks, we don't force a child into a specific growth task until he is mature enough to be ready for the task, but there are some ways to move him toward readiness.

Actually, readiness consists of two dimensions. First, the child has to be physically and emotionally capable of learning and mastering the particular growth mark. Second, the child has to be interested enough to master the task.

Without a ton of sophisticated testing equipment, deciding when a child is physically and emotionally ready is just a matter of judgment. You have studied the child. You have watched him develop. You have worked with him in developing physical skills by playing physical games with him. Through the same games, you have taught him to have the patience it takes to learn by trial and error. Now he is ready to try on his own.

On the other hand, interest can be cultivated. By subtle planning, you might be able to move a child to a position of being interested enough to master the growth mark. Of course, to do this, we need to understand why people are interested in what they are interested in. In other words, where does interest come from?

Educators usually line up on one of two sides in that debate. Some claim interest is a natural thing that springs spontaneously from the child's sense of pleasure and success. Others claim that interest is the result of hard work. If you work at a job long enough, you will get good at it; and once you develop a little competence, you will learn to like it.

Since you have a child at the stage when he is going to be acquiring several new skills and habits during the next few years, you really need to take a few minutes to ponder this question of interest. What do you do? Do you go ahead and buy that violin; then force that six-year-old to stand there in front of a music stand for thirty minutes a day producing all those hideous sounds until he finally learns to make music and love the music he makes? Or do you wait until he comes crawling to you on his hands and knees, begging you for some outlet for his vast musical talents and interests?

Dare we propose a compromise? Perhaps interest is actually the product of imitation. The child sees you do it, and he decides he would like to try. The child decides he would like to read because he sees you reading and enjoying the activity. The child decides he wants to learn to tie a tie because you buy him one. The child wants to learn to play baseball after you take him to a baseball game.

Role modeling is a good teaching technique and imitation is good learning, but teaching through role modeling puts an interesting challenge on the teacher. If you want to promote your child's interest in learning something, you must make sure that what you do is what you want him to imitate.

Of course, timing of many of the growth marks falls into the domain of the school experience. Many of these fit right into the regular schedule, and the child will develop the interest and readiness in the company of his friends and teacher.

In this case, I recommend that unless the child is particularly interested in mastering a specific growth mark, you let him follow the schedule. If your child really wants to read at four and is actually learning to read on his own, you don't want to discourage him by not helping him; but it is also all right if he doesn't want to learn to read until he starts to school.

When my own children were little, I asked one of the best first-grade teachers I have ever known what she wanted children to know when they first come to school. She said, "They need to know how to use the bathroom." Now there is a growth mark their mother can help them master.

Of course, if your child is not making normal school progress in mastering these growth marks (he is going too fast or too slow), you will want to know why. Get the teacher's opinion and match that against yours. If both of you agree that this is a maturity problem, you'll just have to be patient and learn the art of encouraging your child because he is going to need some cheering up when he sees his peers achieve something he hasn't yet.

However, if you suspect something other than a maturity problem, you may want to seek some special help. There are specialists in almost every area of child development, and some of them seem almost to work miracles. (I have seen speech problems completely eliminated in two visits to the therapist.)

But in the midst of all this, the key is not to panic, to keep everything in perspective of a whole life span, and to know your child well enough that you can judge his growth without comparing him with other children.

How Can Parents Help the Child Achieve and Remember the Growth Marks?

During this time when your child is crossing so many new thresholds, it is important for you to remember the significance of each of these events. These are lifetime accomplishments. They are major moments for the child and should be treated as such.

How you celebrate these growth mark achievements depends on your family rituals for recognizing such events, but in your celebration you should accomplish three goals: 1. Make sure your child realizes that you think the event is a special accomplishment. 2. Make the child's accomplishment a family affair, so that he will be interested in sharing both his successes and failures in the family setting. 3. Give the moment enough attention that the child will carry the memory of the circumstances and details with him the rest of his life. Just to show yourself the value of that, pause now and remember some of the moments from your own childhood. Remember the first time you pulled a tooth or tied your shoes or rode a bike or went to school or rode a horse or went down the "big hill" by yourself. These are pleasant, instructive memories. Don't deny your child the same thrill you have had. Help him make a catalog of such moments so he can recall them when he has children of his own.

What you must remember as you make another mark on the sill each birthday is that it all passes so quickly. Soon that age of newness and frequent growth marks will be painted over, and that once-helpless child will have achieved a level of independence. As you turn loose of him so that he can grow and as you help him move toward independence and self-control, make sure you are both developing a catalog of memories so you won't forget what you both learned during this time of rapid growth.

Chapter 3 at a Glance

1. As you set expectations for your child's growth and accomplishments, recognize his uniqueness and individuality. Some children are ahead of schedule; some are behind.

2. Celebrate your child's first-time achievements such as riding a bicycle or pulling a tooth. These experiences provide us with rich memories throughout life.
3. Rushing a child into a specific task before he is physically or emotionally mature enough to handle it might cause him to develop unusual methods of compensation.
4. If your child is a slow developer, make sure you understand the reasons before you employ methods of correction.

4

The Pains of Letting Go

One of the problems with having your child run through a bunch of these growth marks during his early years in school is that this becomes a constant reminder that he is growing; and I suspect that growth always comes with mixed emotions. On the one hand, we celebrate and jump for joy. On the other hand, in the quieter moments of reflection, we wonder whether either one of us is ready for all that change going on in the name of growth. And change does accompany growth. For one thing, when your child masters any one of the characteristic once-in-a-lifetime growth marks, he at the same time achieves a certain kind of independence. When he learns to tie his own shoes, he simply doesn't need you as much as he once did; and those special moments when you tied his shoes for him and then hugged him for good measure just because you had him close enough are gone forever. Now, if he stands still for a hug, you will have to get close to him for some other reason, and there may not be as many hugs as there were before he learned to tie his own shoes. He has grown, but in the same process both of you have lost something.

I don't know about you, but if I had a six-year-old the prospect of rapid growth would throw me into a state of semiterminal ambivalence. Sure, I want my child to grow. I like to brag about his accomplishments. I like to show him off when company comes. I like to feel good about myself as a parent when I see my child making progress and feeling good about his progress. But I must admit that it is painful to turn him loose and give him the freedom and

41

independence he needs in order to grow. Let's think about some reasons for this ambivalence.

1. We are afraid to give the child room to grow because we are afraid he will fail. Actually, failure is part of growing. Any parent discovers that when the child learns to walk. There is just so much falling down and general clumsiness associated with the process. Most of the time, that falling down doesn't hurt anybody or anything; but some of those falls leave bruises and scars, and even broken furniture and vases. I am sure that any parent who has ever been through this business of watching the child learn to walk wishes there were some guaranteed method for controlling the learning laboratory so the child would only experience the painless falls. But there isn't such a method. Both the child and the parent have to take some risks. That is simply an inherent characteristic of growth. In every aspect of human growth, there is always some implied risk and usually some failure.

When the parent sends his child to that other learning laboratory called school, he probably would like the same kind of guarantee he wanted when the child learned to walk—that there won't be any painful falls, any hurts or failures. But there is no such guarantee. In spite of all the great advice given by all of us who claim to know something about schools and children in schools, and in spite of all your concern and direction as a parent, there just isn't any guarantee that your child will adjust to school, learn to read, develop a whole stable of new friends, and become popular and successful without some trying and painful moments.

So how do you know if he is ready for those times? What are you going to do to help him through those moments? Wouldn't it just be easier to protect him from all the possibilities of hurt? Probably, but then there wouldn't be any growth. So you may as well prepare yourself for the ordeal of permitting your child some room to fail.

One strike against failure is that it is time-consuming. It takes the child's time, and it takes your time. Too often, it would just be quicker to do it yourself than to correct the mess your child is going to make while he is learning. You would really like to introduce your six-year-old to the nightly ritual of doing the dishes, but that means that you would have to teach him how first, and that means that you would have to go through it with him a couple of times. Then you would have to turn him loose with the job by himself a couple of times, and then go in and rewash and redry and rearrange when he goofed up. It might save you a lot of time in the long run for him to master that skill, but right now you really don't have time to let him do it wrong enough times to learn how to do it right. It is just easier to do it yourself.

The other day, a very fine young teacher undertook the chore of teaching me and some others the Japanese art of paper folding. I wound up with as nice looking construction as anybody; but I didn't make a single fold. Every time the teacher came by my table, I had my project so botched up that in utter desperation, she refolded everything for me. My work didn't come up to her standard, and she didn't have the time to teach me through my failure. So she just smiled and folded it for me. If I had been six years old, I think she might have spanked me for goofing up, but I really was trying. Unfortunately, I learned the value of failure, and I learned about the patience it takes to tolerate failure.

Another strike against failure is that it is emotion-consuming. When your child gets hurt physically or emotionally, you have to stop what you are doing to patch him up. That not only takes time, but it also wears you both out. No caring parent can be happy when he knows his child is hurting, so during the period following failure, you have to work especially hard at understanding the full complexity of your child. A happy child is a rather simple little being. He carries his happiness and his reasons for his happiness right out in front so everyone can see them. But a sad child, a hurting child, a child despondent over a sense of failure is complex; and the parental task of applying the soothing salve to the hurt is compounded because of those complexities. Why is he hurt? Why does he respond that way when he is hurt? What is the damage of that failure? How quickly should I persuade (is that a nice word for "force") him to tackle that growth mark again? When he almost drowns, how quickly do I put him back into the pool? What can I say or do to help him forget or accept his failure? Should I just leave everything alone and let him grow through the experience? These are tough questions, and the pursuit for answers is an emotionally consuming chase. My life as a parent would be simpler if both the child and I could just forget about his taking the risks necessary to grow. Oh, the pains of turning loose!

A third strike against failure is that it often requires parents to think like children, and that is a tough order. For us to understand failure, we have to look at the undertaking through the child's eyes. We have to define success in his terms and not ours.

I was visiting a young father when his seven-year-old daughter and her friend came in, dragging some old, rotten boards they had dug out of a neighbor's trash.

"May we borrow your saw?" the daughter asked.

"What for?"

"We are going to make a dollhouse," she announced.

"Well, why don't you wait until I am finished and I will get you some better boards. I will help you and we will make a good-looking dollhouse," the father offered.

It was clear that his suggestion didn't please either of the young girls. They went back outside to play and soon forgot their urge to build a dollhouse. Obviously, the two parties were at cross purposes. The father was seeing the prospect of a product, and anything that fell short of his idea of the product would have been a failure. On the other hand, the girls were seeing the prospect of the process. They really didn't care what the dollhouse looked like. The fun and the success were in the making, not in having a finished product. Any dollhouse would have met their standards, so long as they had built it themselves. To understand failure and success, sometimes parents have to think like children. That may be one of the hardest tasks of giving the child enough freedom for him to master these growth marks. Although you may be convinced that he can make his printed letters better, they might have looked rather good to him. He might really have been satisfied with the task until you told him that he had failed.

Nevertheless, failure is definitely a part of growing, and if our children are going to grow, we are going to have to give them the freedom and the support to fail.

2. We are afraid to give the child room to grow because we are afraid he will lose his innocence.   First, let's begin this business of being a parent with an honest admission. Most of us—probably all of us—like people at one age better than we like them at another. Notice, I didn't say anything about love. Parental love is a constant. You will always love your child regardless of what hideous stage he may be going through at the moment. But there will be times when you won't like him as much as you do at other times.

I think many of us like little children—the spontaneous show of affection, the honesty, the innocence, the loyalty, the attention they give to us as parents because of their inability to fulfill their own needs. And somehow we know that as the child grows in size and capabilities some of that will be lost. Since we can't predict what the child of the future is going to be like, we tend to want to cling to the one we have now. We like this one. We would just as soon keep him this way as long as we can. Our child's growth potential does demand some faith on our part. We have to turn loose of the person we have and know and love, and trust God for the unknown person he is going to become.

3. We are afraid to give the child room to grow because we don't want to admit that we are growing into another stage of life ourselves. I probably didn't believe this or even recognize it as a problem until the last of our three children reached school age, but one day Mary and I both awoke to the sobering fact that we were out of babies. That part of our lives was over. Not only was our baby growing past a stage, but so were we. Shopping for Christmas presents became a new venture. We just didn't feel at home in toy stores anymore. Just about the time I got really good at doing distinctive voices for each of the three bears, my audience learned to read and didn't need me anymore. We even got kicked out of the young parents' class at Sunday school. Middle age became a reality all too soon.

We responded to that awful truth with dignity. We tried to keep our last child a baby much longer than we had the others. We just didn't turn loose. We didn't welcome the growth marks with as much celebration as we should have. We didn't give her as much independence. We tried as long as we could to avoid the reality of our own need to grow. Finally, we gave in. We had to. She got her own job, her own driver's license, and her own set of friends, activities, and aspirations. So now we sit in Sunday school with all those middle-aged folks and tell ourselves that we really don't look that old. Oh, the pain of turning loose of our children!

Regardless of the thrill that comes when your child loses a tooth or learns to ride a bike, there still may be something in you that protests the process in progress. That is fairly normal. But you have to deal honestly with those feelings, and someday you have to turn loose. In fact, someday you are even going to have to let another authority into his life, and that is another frightening prospect.

Chapter 4 at a Glance

1. Growth is a process of trial and error. In order to grow, your child has to have the freedom to experiment.
2. During this period of intense growth, your child will fail as often as he succeeds. You need to develop the patience to accept his failure and the skill of encouraging him to keep trying.
3. As your child grows and becomes more independent, your relationship with him changes. You must grow as the child grows.
4. Avoid the urge to do the task for him when you want to save time.

5

Sorting Through the Authority

When your child starts to school, he will meet another measure of growth—new sources of authority. If yours is a fairly normal home, for the first time in his life your child will have to learn to adjust to another adult directing his activities—he will have to adjust to another source of authority. And he will encounter several additional sources of authority during those first three years in school. Now, I don't want to put so much emphasis on this new experience that you feel like hiding your child in the closet, but I do want to make the point that this initial adjustment to those other sources of authority in the child's life is an important time which will have implications throughout his growing years. You need to spend some time thinking about this. First, let us look at some of the possible problems that could mar this experience of starting to school.

Possible Problems

1. For the first time in his life, your child will have to submit to an authority who earned the office by some virtue other than love. First-grade teachers around the world will argue with this point, but let them argue. I am still right. If you love your child (and I suspect you do or you wouldn't be reading this book), he surely feels that love. Consequently, when you advise him or correct him or praise him, he knows that this advice and correction and praise were given out of love. He may not be able to identify that love, but acts of love are known through feelings rather than through words anyway.

The teacher probably loves your child too, but in a more impersonal way. So when the teacher advises or corrects or praises, the child has to understand some other context for that authority. It just isn't the same as when it comes from a parent. So what gives the teacher the right to this authority? Although the child may never be able to understand this in so many words, he still has to be able to sense it. Somehow he has to sense why adults other than his parents have a right and an obligation to order him about. Then, just about the time he decides he can accept the teacher, he meets the teacher aide, the principal, the janitor, the school nurse, the tester, the lady in the lunchroom; and now he is thrown into a whole new dilemma of knowing which adults have authority for specific areas of his life. This is a critical time in a child's development. How he learns to respond to the roles of authority when he first meets them will have a great bearing on how he adjusts to school, how he adjusts to the whole learning arena, and how he adjusts to various sources of authority he will encounter during that time in his life when he must rely heavily on authority for what he is to do and even for what he is to believe. This leads us to the second problem.

2. You will have to have a clear understanding about how you want your child to respond to authority. As a teacher, I can assure you that there is no guarantee that he is going to come out exactly as you want him to. In the process of creation, the Infinite Mind saw fit to give the child some voice in this matter. In other words, God made him an individual. But you need to know what lessons you are trying to teach your child. Also, since those lessons are most forcibly taught through modeling, you must understand how you respond to authority. Do you want and do you teach your child an unquestioned acceptance of every adult's advice or correction, or do you want and do you teach your child a more reasonable approach? That is, consider the source, think through the evidence, and make a rational decision about which authority he will accept and which he will ignore. Or, do you teach your child to fight against all authority, responding to nothing except his own conscience? Again, let me assure you that just in the process of living and being, you are teaching your child one of those positions (or perhaps some combination of all three). But you are nevertheless teaching him to respond to authority in some way. Although he may not do it your way, you must be sure that the message you are communicating is the one you want your child to learn.

3. For the first time in his life, your child may meet conflicting authority. Let's suppose, for example, that you are from the old school which believes little children should refer to adults with some form of formality. About the time you get this message across to your six-year-old, he starts to school, and the first-grade teacher wants to be called Sally. Now what does he do? What do you do? For months you have been pumping this child up to accept the authority of his teacher, and now she contradicts you. This may call for a scene. You can begin with your child. You can try to explain Sally's peculiar idiosyncrasy, telling him that some adults may prefer the first name but all adults will accept the titled last name. If you are good at explaining, and your child is good at accepting, this may suffice. But I doubt it. When one is six years old there is something rather romantic and brazen and grown-up about calling some adult, particularly an adult with authority, by his or her first name. Don't be surprised or disappointed if your child seems to like the idea.

So now you have two options. You can insist and you can go see Sally. You do have a right to both. You have a right to insist that your child accept your principles of authority. You may have to insist several times before he gets the message; but usually, if the matter is significant enough to justify confrontation in the first place, it is worth your effort to keep reminding the child of your rules until he remembers them.

On the other hand, I urge you to go see the teacher. As a parent, you must realize and affirm that all those other adults and adult authorities in your child's life are your helpers in the enterprise of getting your child through childhood and adolescence and into adulthood. They are helpers—nothing more; and they gain the right to their authority by your implied permission. These helpers must understand that they are helpers. They don't have the principal responsibility in this endeavor. They only have the child for a limited time, so they must work within the framework of a much broader scheme. So long as your agenda for your child is not immoral or illegal, those helpers have to honor your program. As a teacher, Sally has to understand that, and you may have to remind her. If she doesn't believe you, tell her to call me and I will tell her. Teachers must honor the parents' wishes for their children so long as those wishes are based on sound judgment and human decency and do not disrupt the classroom climate.

Of course, I use the story of Sally only as an illustration. This problem of conflict of authority in your child's life can rear its ugly head in several places. If you are a thinking parent, trying to rear your children according to the principles of Scripture, you are going to meet this problem frequently. For example, Halloween has always been a source of frustration for our family and for several families who feel as we do about such things. What do you say to a seven-year-old just after you have told him that he cannot go trick-or-treating regardless of what all the other kids, and the teacher, are doing that night?

Every family has its own rituals, its own cultural rules, its own agenda, its own value structure; and when your child first wanders out into the bigger world away from the security of that limited culture, he is going to bump into some conflicting rules. You will have to help him manage those.

4. *At this age, your child will look to authority not only to tell him what to do and how to behave, but also to tell him what to believe.* This is simply the way the human belief structure works for most of us. When we are young, we believe what we do because our accepted authority told us to believe it. Later, we will probably question that authority, and then we will reaffirm those beliefs on a different basis. But for a while, those beliefs by authority serve us well.

Usually, your child will accumulate a whole trunk full of those during his first three years in school. He will develop some strong personal beliefs about such things as his own ability and potential. He will develop some beliefs about his country and his duty to country and fellowman. He will develop some beliefs about the value of education and the definition of success. And, if he has been reared in a typical evangelical home, he might initiate a personal relationship with his Savior.

Those are some rather serious beliefs he is picking up at the same time he is trying to sort through all those sources of authority which have just entered the picture. During this time, your child is going to need you to help him coordinate all the active advice and all the models he is getting so he can form a healthy attitude toward authority.

As I said earlier, this age is a time of abrupt and often forced growth. Suddenly meeting all that variety of authority is just one of those marks your child will have to achieve. But you can help him. I offer some suggestions in the next chapter.

Chapter 5 at a Glance

1. If your child learns to respect authority, he will have to learn it at home. Schools aren't equipped to teach that lesson.
2. Since children learn from consistency and repetition, apply these two principles in teaching your child how to respond to authority. There is nothing wrong with having to remind a child to remember his manners. Someday he will get the message.
3. Since children learn by imitation, teach respect for authority by example. Be careful; your child is watching you.
4. Often, the different authorities in your child's life will not have the same expectations. This is a problem that has to be worked out among the adults. Go see the person with whom you have the conflict and achieve some kind of understanding.

6

Teacher as Authority

When your child reaches the age at which he needs to learn how to manage other sources of authority in his development, the most conspicuous form of that authority will be his own teacher. So I will concentrate the following list of suggestions on how you can help your child adjust to the new experience of having a teacher in his life. Of course, if your child is likely to encounter other adults in large doses, you can use the same suggestions. You will just have to substitute another term for teacher.

Prepare Your Child for Meeting the Teacher Before School Starts

Although some children seem to be excited about school before they come out of the crib, I suspect most have some apprehensive moments as the time draws closer, even those who don't admit it. You can help your child handle those apprehensions by remembering to be positive about school as often as you can; but that may be tougher advice than it sounds. It is rather easy to be negative about school without really meaning to. Or, at least, it is easy for our children to interpret what we say as negative. While you and your friends sit around and reminisce about the pranks you pulled and the times you got into trouble with teachers for such major crimes as chewing gum or talking out of turn, your poor preschooler is listening and developing a bag full of doubts about the whole process.

Also, it is often quite easy to develop the habit of threatening a preschooler with the prospect of school. We do that with such statements as "Sit still while I read to you. When you start to school, your teacher will not like you if you don't sit still." "It's all right to watch that television program now, but when you start to school you will just be too busy to watch every day." "You have to give up that filthy blanket before you start school. What would your teacher think of you with such a thing dragging behind?" "What do you think your teacher would say if she knew you wet the bed? You would be the laughingstock of the whole class."

If I were a five-year-old looking forward to the twelve-year venture into the unknown I could get enough of that kind of talk in a hurry. I realize your need to correct your child and help him develop good habits, and I realize that as parents we often in desperation resort to the last resort; but we need to be aware of the possibility of instilling in our children a sense of fear rather than a sense of trust even before they meet the object of their concern.

On the positive side, there are some definite things you can do. For emphasis (positive reinforcement?), I will list these in a straight line to give you the idea of a checklist so you can tick off what you have done.

1. During story-telling time, tell exciting tales about the good times you had in school.
2. Tell your child about your favorite teacher. In fact, why don't you sit down with your child and write your favorite teacher a letter thanking her for her inspiration and efforts. (I warn you. I am sneaky. But it wouldn't hurt you to remember; it would warm the heart of your favorite teacher; and it would help your child feel positive about the teacher's role in his life.)
3. When you help your prewriter draw pictures of his future teacher, make her a smiling, happy person.
4. Help your child look forward to school by planning some exciting family activities to celebrate the event. In fact, if you

want to do a good job of this, make a whole list of things that you and your child can do during every year of his school career. During first grade, you will read the Narnia Chronicles together. During second grade, you will build a model city together. During third grade, you can make a collection of pictures of state capitol buildings. During fourth grade, he gets to start guitar lessons. You get the idea. Although you may want to keep your list fairly flexible, at least you can see the value of building some anticipation for the event of another year. This may not help your child enjoy third grade at school any more, but it will at least give him something to look forward to. This activity is particularly important for the child who for some reason doesn't like school very much. The threat of twelve years of doing something he either doesn't enjoy or doesn't do well could be depressing.

5. If you know of a child a year or so older than yours who is enjoying school, invite him over and engage him in conversation about his school experiences. This will help your child develop some sense of trust for the teacher.

6. Help your child understand the differences in people. This may be a rather difficult teaching assignment, but you can point out to him that people have different demands and reactions. Use illustrations from friends and family. This will help him adjust to those various authorities he will meet during the school day.

Get to Know Your Child's Teacher and Make Sure Your Child's Teacher Knows You

This isn't double-talk. In fact, I thought about making these two separate items. It is important for you to know your child's teacher. Know what she is like, what her values are, what motivates her, what amuses her, what angers her, and how she responds to various situations. Since you are turning your child over to this helper for about a third of his waking hours, you have every right to know these things about that helper. You need to know, not only for your own peace of mind but so you can assist and supplement when necessary.

At the same time though, that helper (teacher) needs to know those same things about you. You wouldn't hire an assistant to help you with your life's number one project without giving that person some orientation. In the same way, that teacher needs to know you so she can help you in the mission of rearing your child. Don't keep her in the dark. Make sure she knows who you are and what you expect.

Of course, there are good ways, and not-so-good ways of doing this. I suggest you try the good ways first.

1. Go to school and meet the teacher on her turf. See her in person. Sit down and chat for a few minutes. You don't have to be conspicuously frank during that first meeting. If she is any student of psychology at all (and how else could she have made it through teacher training), she can make some observations and read between the lines. She will discern what you feel is important. Also, make sure your child knows you are conversing. In fact, I recommend having the child present at teacher conferences. This way the child will get the idea that the teacher and parent respect each other, and he will be more open to accepting both authorities in his life.

2. Invite the teacher to your house or to a restaurant so she can meet you on your turf. Turnabout is fair play. Of course, this suggestion comes from the teacher part of me instead of the parent part, but there is great possibility here. With salaries what they are in most places, many teachers would appreciate an invitation to a free lunch or an after-school snack. This will give your child the opportunity to see the authorities in his life sit informally and chat about such profound topics as soufflé recipes and Superbowl scores. Any friendly conversation between you and your child's teacher could have an enormous effect on his attitude toward the teacher and his whole approach to learning. Don't deny yourself this rather simple method of enhancing your child's school experience.

3. If you have some extra time, see if you could spend some of it at school on a regular basis. Many schools have developed various programs for encouraging volunteer help; so if your school has such a program, volunteer. If it doesn't have such a program, suggest one. Don't hide behind your feelings of inadequacy. You can help supervise the lunchroom or listen to second graders read or do some filing for a teacher. This is something for you to do. Besides the value you will be to the school and the children you help, your own child will get the idea that you approve of school and what is happening to him.

Demonstrate for Your Child a Positive Attitude Toward Authority

We have research and biblical admonition telling us that what parents do, children repeat—maybe not in every case, but in enough cases to be sobering. Look, if you are going to yell at referees and cops and bosses, don't expect too much different from your child. If you want your child to respect authority, demonstrate it for him. You can be subtle here.

1. Always refer to your child's teacher with the formal title (even if you draw a Sally fifteen years younger than you.)
2. When you are talking with the teacher in front of your child, try using terms of respect. Don't make a big deal of it. Your child will hear you.
3. Sometime when your child is old enough to know what's going on, stop a policeman and ask for directions. Even if you don't need directions, stop and ask anyway. You don't have

to make a speech or issue a paper about respect. Just stop and
ask. Your child will get the message.
4. Respect your child's other parent. (Whoops, that's a different
book.)

Starting and settling into school is an exciting, tedious, happy,
frightening time, both for the people doing it and those helping
them get through it. Growing is always an exciting business, but
we must always remember that as we grow into something, we
also grow out of something, and the give-and-take inherent in
growth is probably never more obvious than during that time
when you and your child learn to manage the other authorities in
his life. But that management is essential in the process of formal
schooling.

Chapter 6 at a Glance

1. Before your child starts school, help him form a positive image
   of school. Speak of your happy times. Create pictures of warm,
   friendly teachers.
2. Establish a working relationship with your child's teacher.
   This will require some time, but the dividends make it worthwhile.
3. Don't let your child see your conflicts with his teacher. Keep
   those private.
4. If your child fears school, you may need to spend some time at
   school yourself. If possible, work in a volunteer program a few
   hours per week. This way, the child will get a sense that you
   approve.

7

Learning at School and Other Paradoxes

After considering all the kinds of growth your child is going to experience during those first three years in school, including adjusting to several different sources of authority, we come to a rather obvious point: School is a unique experience. There is really nothing quite like it. Of course, after a student has been around for a few years, he will probably become so used to the whole routine that he forgets that it is all that different from anything else, but it is still different. And as your child begins the experience, you must be aware that it is different.

Some people have called school a false experience. In fact, some educational experts who always want to change things make a big deal of that point. They tell us that young people don't learn as much as they should because school is a false experience. "If it were real," these change artists prophesy, "students would have such a natural desire to learn that they would plunge into their studies so enthusiastically that all the educational problems would be solved."

Although I realize that it is unique, I am reluctant to call school a false experience. It may seem false to some adult who only visits on rare occasions, but to a young person who is investing about a third of his waking hours in the place, school is reality. For him this *is* the real world. For many children, school demands so much time and attention that it becomes the center of their entire world.

Consequently, as a parent of a school-age child, you must understand how the school experience is unique in the whole realm of human experience and how this unique experience dominates much of your child's time and emotions.

My purpose in this chapter is primarily to ask you for understanding. I will make a few definite suggestions, but the most significant suggestion is that you simply try to understand what your child is going through as he begins his school experience and adjusts to the uniqueness of the whole endeavor. To help you, I list some characteristics that make school a unique experience.

1. The whole environment is different. Since I will break this point down and develop it more fully in later chapters, let me just remind you that school demands five hours of alertness; school demands social interaction; school demands conformity to rules and regulations; school restricts physical movement and demands that someone learn something. I could go on endlessly, but this incomplete list should get you to start thinking about how you will prepare your child for his new environment.

2. School starts the child on the intellectual journey of decoding the symbols of culture. If this sounds like so much educational gobbledygook let me illustrate. In his play about Helen Keller, *The Miracle Worker,* playwright William Gibson portrays the young Helen as a wild, untamed animal running through life in a girl's body. Through the serious efforts of a determined tutor, Annie Sullivan, there is little progress. But in the final, poignant scene, Helen, in a fit of rage, learns the meaning of the word *water.* According to the playwright, this is the first time the girl catches the idea that a word actually refers to some element of reality. From this perception, she immediately starts on the road to culture and intelligence. Of course, this whole process has been condensed for the sake of dramatic effect, but it does give us an insight into what happens in a child's mind as he grows intellectually.

When the child is very young, he knows real things. He knows the things he can touch and see and feel. But somewhere in the process, he begins to realize that certain symbols represent those real things. Words are symbols. The word *water* is not a reality. It is only the symbol representing the stuff that runs out of the glass, down my chin, and stains my tie. The number 4 is not a real thing. It is only a symbol of whatever it is you happen to be counting at the moment.

The whole concept of intelligence, at least as educators and psychologists use the term, is based on the mastery of those symbols. The more symbols a person knows, the higher he scores on the intelligence test. Your child's future options depend on his becoming comfortable with his task of decoding the symbols.

Of course, this process begins before the child starts to school. Very early, he begins to learn the meaning of oral symbols. In other words, he learns to talk, and perhaps to sing, and perhaps to interpret a musical tone on an instrument. When he starts to school, he has to manage a whole new system of symbols—written symbols such as letters, numbers, words, and musical notes. He has to learn that these things represent reality just as he learned how oral symbols communicated reality for him in the earlier language stages.

This transition from oral to written decoding is a complex activity. Some children manage it better than others, but all need some help and understanding. Since I will make specific suggestions in later chapters when I deal with activities such as reading, writing, and doing arithmetic, here I will say only that you can help your child by remembering that he may need to go back to the reality in order to understand the meaning of the symbol.

We have a whole storehouse of stories about those times when adults said one thing, but children heard something else. I suspect that almost all young Sunday school students once sang about Gladly, the cross-eyed bear. A kindergarten teacher told me about the girl who drew Round John Virgin in her nativity scene. The Irish teacher thought she detected something amiss in the class's recitation of the Twenty-third Psalm, so she listened as several of the children soberly proclaimed, "And good Mrs. Murphy will follow me all the days of my life."

It is a strange world, this world of verbal and written symbols all carrying some tidbit of information about reality to our brains. And if we goof up on one of the minor points, we could get the wrong impression (mental picture). Your child needs at least your understanding as he makes this transition into the written code. As he begins the process of reading, counting, making sense of arithmetic computation, or creating a musical sound equivalent to a note on a sheet of paper, he needs some very close supervision to remind him of the reality represented by these symbols he is working with.

To remember how this process works, it might help to play "Let's remember when we learned something specific." When I was in the first grade, I overheard my teacher assess a pan of liquid as "half-full." I thought that was a neat term so I registered it in my conscious storehouse of words. A few days later, my father asked me to climb on his tractor and tell him how much gas was left in the tank. I was so thrilled because I got to practice my new word—*half-full*. With that reassurance, he drove merrily off, prepared to plow for several hours. A short time later, he came walking home for more fuel. That night he took a bucket and some water and taught me the real meaning of my new symbol. To this day, I still know what *half-full* means.

Remembering this incident helped me to understand what was happening to my children when they began the process of decoding the cultural symbols of reality.

**3. *Learning is a private, personal activity put into a public arena in
school.*** One of the first things you must understand as you send
that six-year-old off to school is the private character of learning.
Learning is a very intimate, personal process which demands
from all learners a certain degree of vulnerability. In order to
learn, we first have to admit that we are inadequate, incomplete.
That makes sense. If we were all perfect, there would be no need
to learn. But before we can learn, we have to expose our inadequacy. We have to expose that inadequacy to those who propose
to teach us; and if there are others around, such as in the classroom, we have to go through the agony of exposing our ignorance
to them as well. I, personally, am not very comfortable with that
prospect. I don't mind being dumb, but I hate to submit that piece
of information to public knowledge. So I guard my ignorance
with a passion. Am I any different from a normal second
grader?

Also, learning is frequently an activity of trial and error. If we
get it wrong the first time, we have to be emotionally prepared to
keep trying until we get it right. That prospect alone is frightening
enough; but when I think about the possibility of getting it wrong
in front of twenty-seven of my classmates, I get weak knees. I can
understand how students earn such teacher comments as "unco-
operative," "inattentive," or even "lazy." It may be easier for the
child to adopt one of those behaviors than to submit himself to
the vulnerability it takes to learn in a school setting.

Fortunately, there are some things parents can do to help the
child adjust to learning in public. Let me list some.

1. Make sure your child has some friends in his classroom. Since
school learning takes place in a social context, the more comfortable the student is with that environment, the better equipped he
will be to accept the vulnerability required to learn. He needs
friends beside him. You can manage this. Find out who is in his

class (the school will provide you with those names) and invite some students and their parents over to your house so the children can play together before school starts. I suspect that those parents will be happy to cooperate when they find out why you are doing this.

2. If your child will be riding a bus, make sure he knows someone on the bus before school starts. I still find riding a bus a rather frightening experience. Knowing someone helps me overcome my feeling of exposure.

3. Make sure your child knows his teacher before school starts. If that isn't possible, make sure the teacher and your child have a face-to-face conversation on one of the first days of the new school year. How do you engineer that? Easy! Make an appointment to pick up your child from his classroom on one of the first days of school. Thus, you will get to meet the teacher, you will get to see the room, and you can arrange a moment when your child and the teacher talk face to face.

4. If your child will be walking to school, help him get familiar with the route before school starts. Walk with him. Comment about landmarks and potential dangers. And this is not just a suggestion for parents with first graders. Continue this practice with your child for several years. This will help give him a sense of anticipation for the coming year, and it should lessen his fear of learning in an unfamiliar setting.

5. Visit your child's classroom often enough so that you will be able to relate his tales of school to specific scenes and people. When he tells you about Jason marking up the bulletin board, you will be able to visualize the crime.

6. *Play competitive games with your child.* I don't want to get into an argument about the pros and cons of competition here, but I do want to convince you of the need to teach your child the frustration and joy of learning by trial and error. Competitive games, particularly board games, will help him get there. He will learn to accept himself when he is less than perfect. Thus, he will be able to preserve his dignity while he has to try a task several times.

7. *Don't be afraid to let your child see your vulnerability.* Don't be afraid to admit how many times you have learned by failing and retrying.

8. *Accent the positive.* As much as is possible, make your child comfortable about being himself apart from what he does. Assure him of his value. In fact, make that a daily event during those first three years of school. He may be having a particularly frustrating time trying to master something, and your assurance may be the thing he needs to keep him trying. Make him realize that he is not a bad person just because he isn't learning something as quickly as some others.

9. *Make a big deal of his accomplishments.* I know I said that earlier, but it bears repeating here.

School life provides each individual a unique experience. The environment is different from the home; the purpose is unusual; and at times learning in a social setting seems almost contradictory to the basic characteristic of learning itself. That is why it is so important that you understand what is demanded of your child during those first three years when he is adjusting to this unique enterprise.

In the next few chapters, we will look at some other paradoxes that make school such a remarkable experience for the beginning learner.

Chapter 7 at a Glance

1. Starting school is often more of an abrupt change in the child's life than we adults realize. You need to help your child handle that change.
2. Arrange for your child to spend some playtime with his classmates.
3. Encourage the child to talk about school events. Let him know that you are interested in that part of his life. This way, you will make the experience real for him.
4. As your child makes the transition into a world of written symbols, he will make some mistakes in perception. Don't overreact to those mistakes and discourage him.

8

The Dependent/Independent
Paradox

Do you remember when you were young and said such things as, "When I have children of my own I will never run them around in circles telling them to get permission to do something from the other parent." "I will never give an order without a reason." "I will always answer when they ask why." "I will never compare a child with his brothers or sisters." "I will never tell a child one day that he is too old for irresponsible behavior, then tell him the next day he is too young to be trusted with responsibility."

Oh well, being a parent is far more humbling than planning to be one. We can't all be perfect.

But we do confuse the child with a dependent/independent paradox during that time when the child is first making his adjustment between home and school. It is quite possible that the authorities in his life don't always agree on how much of his own life and decision making he is capable of handling at that particular time. At home, he may get the idea that he is still a child, needing constant supervision and protection; while at school he may feel that he has a lot of adult responsibility in such things as taking care of his own possessions and managing his own time. Or it may be the other way around. He may get the idea that he is trusted at home, but not trusted at school. Or he may even get the idea that both teachers and parents seem to trust him with some matters of responsibility but don't trust him with others. It may not even occur to the adults that they are projecting this confusion, but it can be very disconcerting to the average eight-year-old.

The whole matter deserves some of your time for evaluation. It is not so much a question of asking if you are expecting too much or too little from your child; it is more a question of whether you and the other authorities in his life are consistent with what you do expect.

Do you pin notes on his shirt or expect him to be responsible enough to get the message to the right person? At what age do you allow him to handle telephone messages? Do you check to see if he ate his lunch, or do you leave that to his own choice? How do you send his fees to school? When do you give him a key to the house? At what age is he responsible enough to stay home without a baby-sitter? Do you trust him to do his homework or do you make sure every day? What do you do when he loses something? To what degree is he responsible for the way he looks—clothes, hair, nails?

There are actually two goals to work toward. First, you want to make sure you don't give the child so much independence or responsibility that you frustrate him or drive him to compensate by acting more grown-up than he really is. But at the same time, you want to give him enough responsibility that you challenge him to continue to grow toward becoming a responsible person. Knowing what that proper amount of independence or responsibility is may be one of the toughest tasks of parenthood. My oldest daughter is twenty-four and has been married for two years, but I am still wondering if she is mature enough to handle her life. Somehow the parental urge to protect gets in the way when we think about giving a child some room for a little independence.

Although I don't have any suggestions about how to manage a consistency of expectation during this time when the child is so likely to meet the different levels, I do have some suggestions that can help you help him adapt to growing independence; and by growing more independent he is more likely to adjust to the varying levels of expectations.

1. Give your child some chores.   If you live on a farm with horses and chickens and cows and a garden, that is a rather simple suggestion; but if you are a typical suburban parent, chores are a little tougher to find. This may be the biggest challenge of child rearing to the suburban or urban parent. Where are we going to get enough chores, responsible chores, to help our children grow into responsible people? Where are we going to find enough significant work to teach our children that the work must be done? Sometimes we have to look deep and be creative. You may want to buy a family pet to provide some added responsibility! You may need to take a hard look at all those labor-saving devices you have been wanting. In our town we get somewhere between 30 and 100 inches of snow a year. For several years I have wanted a snowblower. I can even afford to buy one. But I will not buy one as long as I still have children at home. Shoveling is a family task. We all must assume the responsibility for keeping the walks clean. I have even come to the point where I actually thank God for snow.

Actually, doing chores teaches a child many things. Obviously, it teaches him to handle responsibility and independence. But it also helps him get the message that he is an important person. He is making some contribution to the world. He is worthwhile while he is still growing. These are important lessons, and they are worth teaching. They are worth teaching in spite of all the protests you may get from your child. Persist. Demand. Expect. The end result is worth the determination it may take to get there.

2. Expect your child to do the chores.   Bear with me. I am about to say something controversial here. I believe it is important that we teach a child to do these chores for no other reason than we expect him to do them. I am not too ecstatic about the practice of paying a child some fee for every little bit of work he performs around the house. I do understand the need to teach a child the value of work and the idea that money comes from work. But I believe more strongly in teaching the child the importance of necessity: "For now, you do the job because it has to be done. There will be time for those other lessons later and in a different context. You do the job because you are old enough to assume some responsibility for your own being. You do the job because I expect you to do it."

I have heard the children ask, "What will you give me if I do it?" It seems to me that is the same question as, "What will happen to me if I don't do it?" I think both are dangerous questions. In the child's mind, the reward or the punishment is more important than the responsibility. He is not learning much about independence from this kind of question.

I have been around children in huge quantities for more than twenty-five years, and the one thing I have come to believe with the greatest conviction is that children usually do what is expected of them. I even have tons of research to support that conviction. If you assign your child some chore and expect him to do it, sincerely expect him to do it, he will have learned something about responsibility and independence; and you may even be surprised at his capability.

3. Start your child on some kind of allowance as soon as he is able to count money. No! That is not contradictory to the point above. These are two different suggestions. Don't make the allowance circumstantial. He gets the money regardless of whether he does his chores. (We will get to this possibility in the next point.) The amount of the allowance is not all that important. Don't worry if you can't afford very much (and don't be embarrassed if your child's friend gets twice as much). The important thing here is the lesson not the money. But give the child the allowance and help him work out a budget (include the tithe and other essentials), and expect him to stick to it. You may be pleasantly surprised at how quickly your child grows into some responsible attitudes.

4. Make your child responsible for his own actions.   When he fails to do something he should have done, or he does something he shouldn't have, handle the situation in such a way that he suffers the consequences of his own action. This is actually more difficult than spontaneous punishment. If he doesn't do his chores, don't spank him or withhold his allowance. That would be too easy! Make him do his chores. Take the word of experience here. If you wake an eight-year-old out of a warm bed to carry out the garbage at 1:00 A.M. he probably won't forget next week. Spanking him would have been easier, but it wouldn't have taught him the lesson you wanted him to learn.

There is actually a higher-level suggestion implied in this. Don't punish the child; punish the action. In other words, when it is possible, make the punishment grow out of the action. This way, the child will get the idea that you approve of him. You just don't like what he did.

5. Make your child responsible for his own possessions and environment.   Occasionally, I hear about some mother who discovers disturbing material while cleaning her child's room. I sympathize with that mother, but I wonder why she was cleaning the room in the first place. I hope she was just snooping.

As any teacher will tell you, a child old enough to read and write is old enough to keep his own room clean. He may need a little supervision or occasional help, or he may even have to be told when his idea of cleanliness falls below acceptable standards; but the child should be given the bulk of the responsibility for keeping his room clean. As I have said frequently, it might be easier to do it yourself than to persist; but the child needs the joy of being responsible for his own affairs.

This same lesson applies to possessions. Except for such things as clothes, which require special attention, the child needs the responsibility of managing his own property. He must be aware of where things belong, and he needs to be taught to keep his things in order. If he loses something, he should have to find it. You may want to help him with the search, but the primary responsibility for the hunt should be his. If he destroys something, he should suffer the loss.

These are both personal and social rules. In the school setting, the child will be expected to be responsible in such matters. You can help the teacher manage those thirty students by making sure your child is developing a sense of independence while he is adjusting to school during those first three years. And as he becomes more independent, he will develop self-control.

Chapter 8 at a Glance

1. Children respond differently to the prospect of becoming independent, particularly during this time when they are trying to put together the two worlds of home and school.
2. If your child gets into a pattern of demanding constant direction and supervision, he must learn to trust his own judgment and effort. You can teach him this by developing situations which demand that he work independently.
3. Chores are a good teaching technique because they provide the responsibility of independence and the security of routine.
4. If we give children an extrinsic reward for everything they do

(money, cookies, etc.), they will never learn the joy of completing a task for the thrill of the task.

5. If your child exhibits an unusual show of independence as he begins school, keep the relationship open anyway. He may need to come back for hugs and lap-sitting later.

6. Children usually do what adults expect them to do. But both you and your child have to be clear about those expectations.

9

The Conformity/Creativity Paradox

"They enter first grade as originals and come out of third grade as copies," a teacher told me the other day while she was considering the plight of education. It isn't a very promising possibility is it? I can understand why you have some mixed emotions about sending your child into that strange institution which could strip him of that part of him which makes him so special.

In fact, I can even remember when it happened to me. I was in the third grade at the time. I had just spent the better part of a hot, sweaty afternoon working long multiplication problems; and I was ready for a break, or at the least, a word of encouragement. When I took my paper up to show it to the teacher, she made those overdramatic gestures of displeasure that teachers practice for hours; and she declared, "I just won't accept this. It is entirely too messy. I want you to separate those problems." So I obediently took the paper back to my desk, got out my scissors, and separated those problems for her. That day I learned the penalty for being creative, and I haven't tried it since.

Does school *have* to be such a place? Is there any way that your child can adjust to the rituals and routines of school without losing his identity in the process? Let's hope so. But before we get into a discussion about how to help your child manage the paradox, we should establish some boundaries. Just exactly what is creativity? What are we talking about?

Too frequently when we speak of creativity, we put unnecessary limits on the process. We either get the idea of the child following an elaborate set of instructions to construct some little unusual craft project; or we get the idea of some unstructured, freewheeling, absurd activity no one else can understand. Perhaps we can call both activities creative, but I think it would be unfair to limit the process to either. Without turning this discussion into a deep philosophical debate, I will, for the purpose of this chapter, define creativity as the art of being inventive in thought or action. I realize that definition may be on the same level as defining a ball as a circular object—it really doesn't get us anywhere—but perhaps the definition will make more sense in context. I thought about using the word *original* in the definition, but I am not convinced it is appropriate. I am not sure I know how original any of us are at any time because we probably don't know if we are simply borrowing and adapting an idea we have seen before. Since those ideas might have been lurking in our subconscious, it would be incorrect to call them original. So, I am more comfortable with the word *inventive.* It is the process of taking what we know or what we create and adjusting, extending, or applying it to whatever we are doing. The concept of creativity does suggest that we are doing something out of the ordinary, something unusual; but it does not necessarily imply that we are strange and bizarre. When we are being creative, we may just be putting some unusual twists to standard processes.

So now that we have settled that, we ask ourselves, *Is that kind of behavior not accepted in schools? Is there something about the institution which prevents or discourages a child's creative urges?* I hope not; but at the same time, we have to admit that there are some characteristics about school life which make it a routine. And that routine can become so forceful that it represses creative bents. Let me list some of those characteristics.

1. School demands conformity. Since your child is just one in a class of twenty-five or thirty, it is necessary for him to follow the rules that establish order and sameness in the class. If the teacher wants the child's name in a certain place on the paper, he must learn to put his name there. That not only teaches him to follow instructions, but it makes it easier for the teacher to read the paper. If the teacher wants the children to go to the bathroom in a straight line, your child will just have to learn to be another stick in a line. The whole school decorum demands it. If the teacher wants the books open to page 35, your child will have to have his book open at page 35. This isn't the time for him to be off fulfilling his own impulses to read what he wants to read.

2. School emphasizes learning that can be measured, and we don't have a very good way of measuring inventive thought. Now, let's be honest. We can talk about wanting our children to be creative and inventive, but first I want my child to learn to read and write and count and add. When I go to see the teacher, I want her to tell me how my child is doing in those areas. I don't much want to hear, "Although he can't read halfway through the second-grade level, he does draw the most unusual pictures."

How is he doing in those areas of learning that can be measured? Schools are actually designed to teach those things. Teachers measure their success by how well their students perform in measurable activities. It is not as if schools actually discourage creativity. In fact, some teachers and some schools insist that they put a great deal of emphasis on this part of a student's development. But those learning skills that can be measured are more highly emphasized. We may argue about whether that is the right emphasis and we may even argue about who is to blame for the schools putting this kind of direction on their mission. Perhaps this is what schools do because this is what parents expect them to do. Despite all this arguing, the student is going to spend most of his time and get most of his rewards for learning things that can be tested, measured, and charted on a report card. There just isn't a lot of room for inventiveness in an activity such as spelling.

Of course, this kind of learning is not entirely contradictory to creative development. It just overshadows it in emphasis. In fact, we probably need those basic measurable skills in order to be more creative. We can't really invent a thought or project unless we have some learned base to use as a starting point; so accumulating skills and knowledge will enhance a child's creative potential. But he will need some opportunity to see the prospect of doing something with that potential. He may not see that opportunity emphasized.

3. *School demands a lot of the student's time.* Last week a parent called me to complain about his son's teacher. This parent felt that the teacher assigned so much homework that the child did not have time to explore his own imagination. When the parents consulted her, the teacher was shocked. She thought she was doing the children and, subsequently, the parents a favor by stimulating their intellectual growth.

I am not going to choose up sides in this debate, but I do think every concerned parent should hear it. Homework is valuable, almost indispensable, in the education of your child. If your child is ever going to be completely proficient in such things as reading and computing math, he has to practice those skills outside of school. Regardless of how bright your child is or isn't, there simply is not enough time in school for him to master completely all the knowledge and skills you expect him to master. So on one hand, we thank the teacher for her care in making and marking homework assignments.

On the other hand, some teachers can get carried away with this homework routine. Not all work is good work. Not all work is worthy of the time it takes to do it. Some teachers *do* assign busywork to impress the students and parents.

Creativity needs time of its own. In fact, your child's creative genius may be most active when the rest of his body and mind is goofing off. The great scientist first thought of his important principle while wading through the sand at the beach. The poet created his masterpiece while lying in a rowboat looking at the sky. According to legend, the story of Frankenstein was created by a lady trapped in a cabin during a snowstorm. If these people had been out doing wholesome work, we might never have had those discoveries which enrich our lives.

So now you have another conflict. You really welcome these demands the school will put on your first, second, or third grader, and you appreciate the fact that the teachers care enough to discipline his life, concentrate on his mastering the learning skills, and even encourage him to study at home. At the same time, you want the child to have enough time, enough energy, and enough intellectual freedom to use his mind and hands for activities that can be called creative. You don't want your child to come out of third grade as just another copy.

Obviously, you are going to have to supplement the school in this area. You might wish you didn't have to—that the school would provide your child the stimulus and the reinforcement for his creative development, but I doubt if you can depend on that. If you want your child to develop and sustain his creative urges and impulses, you will have to help him. Of course, in every chapter of this book, I encourage you to supplement the school, but in this area it is particularly critical that you are prepared to help the child at home.

Before I present some very specific activities you can use toward this end, let's review some of the characteristics of creativity.

1. Creativity demands time for reflection and trial and error.
2. Creativity grows out of confidence. When I am feeling inse-
   cure and unloved, I try to do what I think other people expect
   me to do. I try to win acceptance by conforming. But when I
   feel good about myself, I can be experimental; I can be creative. For instance, when I feel confident about my ability with
   the language, then I can be creative with some of the rules of
   the language.
3. Creativity can demonstrate itself in many ways. There doesn't
   necessarily have to be some end product to show that your
   child has been creative. Or the end product can be as unique as
   your child. It may be a poem, a picture, a song, new rules for a
   game, a birdhouse, a model city, or a new way of coming down
   the stairs. These are all creative ventures!
4. Frequently, creative activity is its own purpose. Most of the
   time, most of what we do has some desired end result. Creative
   activity may be its own end. If we are to encourage children to
   be creative, we must understand their standards.

Now that I have convinced you that you will have to supplement the school in helping your child become both disciplined
and creative, let me suggest some activities that you can use to
help your child see the joy in being inventive.

1. Encourage him.   That is the first challenge. Sure, you are prepared to reward him when he achieves some school milestone like
making a good grade in reading or counting to 100 or writing his
name in cursive. I don't blame you. Those things need rewarding.
But also encourage him when he does something outside that
measured realm. And don't wait around until he constructs some
fabulous piece of art. Recognize his uniqueness in the creative
thought.

2. Set some standard.   Before you hang it on the refrigerator
door, make sure it satisfies your child's expectations. Make sure
he is happy with it.

3. Play some games that expand his imagination. You don't even have to be all that creative to think of some of these. Charades is always good because that game requires the child to communicate by using something other than words. (If you have not played Charades, it is actually quite simple. Think of something like a song title, book title, or familiar quotation. The person who is "it" is the only one who knows the title and has to act out the title so the audience can guess. The actor is limited only to gestures and body language. He can't use words.)

Another good game is Brainstorming. Hold up some object and have everybody in the room think of unusual ways that object could be used. For practice, let's try a common household sponge. Quickly now, how could we use that sponge? To drink up the medicine when Mother isn't looking, to hush a certain commentator during the football game, to carry in your pocket so you think you have a wallet full of money when you really don't, put frosting on it and serve it as a cake as a practical joke. Now, you've got the idea.

Twenty Questions is a fun game for those times when you don't have equipment—such as when the family is riding in the car or waiting in the doctor's office. The one who is "it" thinks of a famous person, and the players have a total of twenty yes or no questions to discover the identity.

I hope you are not disappointed that this list of games is not wild and exotic. Sure, these are common games your family probably plays anyway. But I wanted to keep the list simple and everyday because I wanted you to see how easy it is to help your child maintain his creative bent.

4. Do things that will stimulate your child's senses. Just as the game of Charades throws him back on his own initiative by removing his most common means of communication, we can stimulate some of our lazy senses by taking away some of the more active ones. For example, blindfold your child and take him for a walk outside. This will stimulate his senses of touch, hearing, and smell. After you are finished, talk with him about what he remembers. If you haven't done this, try it yourself. It is rather delightful to become acutely sensitive to the gentle breeze blowing against your face or hear a traffic light changing colors. While your child is blindfolded, have him identify a whole assortment of things by touch or by smell. When the blindfold is removed, mouth words but don't make any sound. Thus, he will have to read your lips and hear by watching. For the same practice, teach him to mouth words along with his records.

5. Encourage him to be creative in play. I don't want to sound like an old grouch always championing "the good old days," but we don't always do our children great favors by overloading them with all these latest toys which leave absolutely nothing to the imagination. I still think that a doll who drinks imaginary milk from a make-believe bottle is more fun than one who drinks real liquid from a real bottle; but you may have to teach your daughter that! Creativity is an active process. Some of these toys make our children too passive in play. You don't have to go to the extreme of being guilty of child abuse here, but you can provide your child with simple instruments that he can transform into sophisticated play equipment by his own imagination.

6. Create with your child. Start a story and let him think of the ending. Read a description of a scene, then both of you draw a picture of it. If you suspect he has musical ability or you want him to have musical ability, play a record and let him lead the imaginative orchestra. Draw pictures together. Write stories together. Show him that you still have an imagination despite all your years in school.

7. Help him see the creative side of schoolwork. Show him how reading can lead him into a world of fantasy. Play some fun arithmetic games. Let me give you an example. You probably learned this somewhere, but let me remind you of the process of casting out nines to prove our computation.

$$
\begin{array}{ll}
44 & (\text{add } 4 + 4) = 8 \\
\underline{+32} & (\text{add } 3 + 2) = \underline{5} \\
76 & \phantom{(\text{add } 3 + 2) = } 13 \\
(7 + 6 = 13) \quad (1 + 3 = 4) & (1 + 3 = 4)
\end{array}
$$

Since the two fours match, the problem is correct. (In other words, just keep adding digits until you get to single digits.) Now, try that with subtraction or multiplication. Isn't this fun? Think of the creative person who discovered this little activity. Arithmetic isn't all drudgery.

8. Provide opportunities for your child to be in creative situations with other children.   Encourage him to be in the church play. If he wants to join the orchestra, give him the opportunity.

Of course, this list isn't complete, but it can get you started. From here you can use your own inventiveness to create some games and situations to help your child preserve his own creative urges. There isn't any penalty for being a creative parent.

I do realize that this chapter is based on what might be a controversial assumption—that being creative is a desired virtue for both children and adults who would still like to be children. It might seem that the adult world demands and rewards conformity—that creativity gets in the way of production and success; but I don't agree. None of us knows what God has in store for our children, but I do know that we should do what we can to prepare them to be happy in the circumstances in which they find themselves. I am convinced that a creative person, a truly creative person, spends fewer hours of his life being bored or grumpy. He may not be any richer or more successful or more powerful, but he should be a little more excited about living.

A classic story illustrates this point. A reporter went out to check on the construction of a new church. One craftsman was skillfully sanding beautiful wooden beams for the ceiling. When the reporter asked him what he was doing, he gruffly replied, "I am sanding a beam. What does it look like?"

Next, the reporter spoke with the craftsman assembling the magnificent stained-glass windows. Again, the answer was terse. "I am making a stained-glass window. What does it look like?"

Finally, the reporter stopped the man who had been given the task of sweeping up behind the two skilled craftsmen. "What are you doing?" the reporter asked.

"I am building a temple for the worship of God," the sweeper proclaimed.

I want my child to be the kind of person who builds temples rather than sands beams. I want him to have an imagination big enough to see the truth.

Chapter 9 at a Glance

1. Just as God made us unique creatures, He gave us unique ways of looking at things. Since schools can't always provide a fertile field for cultivating that uniqueness, parents must if the child is to retain it.
2. Creativity demands imagination. In children, imagination occasionally leads to tall tales.
3. The confidence to be creative can be learned by imitation. Can you set your child an example?
4. Imaginative people make unusual experiences out of usual situations. Routine schoolwork can provide for creativity but

most children will need to be taught how. Show your child how to play learning games. For example, help him create his own devices for remembering.

5. A particularly creative, artistic child may find school frustrating. That child will need some outlet for his artistic impulses. If your child is artistic, help him cultivate his gifts and keep his cheerfulness.

10

The Gentle Art of Reading

ΘCℰΛ C ?ℰ||$Cℰ% ℾCℰ ||ἰℰ *& &CVℰ
&△== *&)*β ℾ* #ℰ ||=CVℰ
C *¢ℰΛℰ% +β +CΛ% ℾ* &C== ||
=CVℰ=*Λἰ Λℰℰ%
C =ℰ||?Λℰ% ℾ* ? ℰ||%

(See solution at end of chapter)

Did you enjoy my poetry? Or did you find it frustrating because you couldn't make any sense out of those scratches? I really wasn't trying to upset you, but I did want to remind you of what a child goes through when he breaks over from a nonreading world into a reading world. I wanted to remind you of what it is like to look at a page of written symbols that have to be interpreted before you get the message. This is what reading is all about.

But this little simple process of interpreting and digesting those written scratches is the single most important intellectual activity in the modern world. If your child is ever to become educated, if he is ever to succeed in a world so dependent on such symbols, if he is ever to become an intelligent shopper in the grocery store, if he is ever to develop a personal devotional life based on Scripture, if he is ever to travel on the highways, if he is ever to go places he has never been before, if he is ever going to know the joy of entertaining himself through the pages of a good book, he needs to become proficient at this skill.

Since it is a skill, reading is a learned activity. Most children, with proper instruction, supervision, and encouragement, can learn to read as well as they want or need to read. The rare exceptions are those very special children with learning disabilities that prevent them from performing one of the brain operations required in reading. But if your child is normal, he can learn to read. How well he reads could depend on how well he is taught and encouraged. For this reason, those first three years are crucial for him, for you, and for his teachers. The three of you need to cooperate in this adventure so that your child can master the skill sufficiently to achieve his creative potential. How well your child does during those first three years will have significant impact on how well he does throughout his educational career. To help your child make this transition into a reading world, you need to understand as much as you can about the process of reading. Let me offer some thoughts.

Reading Is Saying Words

At its most fundamental level, reading is saying words. It combines the process of seeing the letters, sounding them out, putting the accent in the right place, and making a word. Of course, as a child improves, he moves through this stage rather rapidly, and the whole process becomes almost automatic for an experienced reader. But it is still a necessary, fundamental procedure.

A few years ago, one of my superiors asked me to read a report he had written. It was a solid piece of work, but the conclusion just didn't make any sense. Finally, the man asked my opinion. I shuddered at the possible consequences of being too honest, and told him what I thought. He acted shocked and only mildly upset; so I asked him to read the conclusion to me. When he read it aloud, it sounded all right. So I checked it again and found the problem—one small word. The word was supposed to have been *now,* and he was reading *now.* He had always read *now,* but instead the typist had typed *not.* That may be a minor difference in spelling, one small letter, but it sure makes a ton of difference in meaning. Regardless of how proficient we become in the skill of reading, we still need to say the words occasionally. You don't want to dwell on this; it is very basic. But you do want to give your child opportunities to read aloud.

Reading Is Imaging

One of the reasons we read is to take the words from the paper and use them to sketch a picture in our minds. When your child sees the word *snake* and says the word *snake,* he draws a picture of a snake in his mind. If he has never seen a snake, he may need some other cues to help him get the picture right. You may have to show him a picture or go into some description. Frequently without those added cues to help guide him to the image, the reader will just skip over the word as if it isn't even there. That is an interesting little tool most of us use occasionally—the ability to skip over a word, either written or oral, for which we don't have the sufficient background to decipher. But it can be a dangerous practice, particularly for a beginning reader.

Imaging through reading is still one of the most rewarding and cheapest pleasures available to us. I will never forget Huck Finn's raft or Heidi's home in the mountains because I built those pictures in my own mind from the words the authors used. Don't disturb me with some movie. My image is too much a part of my memory. I urge you not to cheat your child out of such pleasures. Read to him and let him read to you. Show him how to build those pleasant and memorable images.

Reading Is Receiving Information

One of the functions of reading is to get the facts off the paper and into our brains. Although this is not completely different from imaging, it does require a bit more precision. In imaging, if the word is *dog,* the child can imagine any dog, but if the sentence tells the reader that the basenji doesn't bark, the reader has to be more precise in handling the data. And being precise requires more activity from the reader. Unless the author has been very elaborate with his structure, the reader has to build some structure for grasping and grouping the facts. In order to store the information, he has to put it into some kind of mental package, and usually the reader is responsible for providing that package himself.

When the child begins to read for the purpose of acquiring information, he will probably need some help in such activities as distinguishing between important and unimportant material. He will have to recognize the topic sentence; and he will need some concept of outlining or categorizing. These are rather sophisticated tools for the average eight-year-old.

Reading Is Interacting

When I read: "The word *education* comes from the Latin verb, *educare* meaning 'to lead out'; so the appropriate education is that which leads out of the student what he already knows but doesn't know he knows," I say, "Wait a minute; I am not sure I agree with that. I have some arguments that you will have to answer before I can accept that definition." So I read on to see if the author is smart enough to answer my questions and convince me of his definition. I am interacting with the material.

To become intelligent readers, we must learn to interact with the material. We must learn that all written material is not necessarily true or infallible, that it has to stand the test of our own thoughts and feelings; and we must learn that we have to reject some written material.

Notice that I used the word *learn* in each of the above warnings. I did that on purpose. Interacting is a learned skill that is often a little late in coming. Try walking into a sixth-grade class and announcing that there is a mistake in the students' textbook. That ought to get an argument started in a hurry. "What do you mean, a mistake in the book? Who do you think you are to question the book? I don't care what you say. I am going to memorize it exactly as it is written because that is what the teacher wants on the test." Oh, the protests are endless!

But that kind of reading, reading only for information without interaction, can lead to the very dangerous kind of reading in which we accept at face value everything in newspapers or magazines or even books. Somewhere in his reading development, your child will need to learn to interact with the material.

The four points above constitute my analysis of what happens when we are reading. Although you might get a different approach from someone else, please see my intent. As a parent, you have to understand what is happening in your child's mind as he begins and develops his reading skills. Any analysis of reading can provide you the direction for that understanding, and it can also lead to the next question: What are the steps or stages in learning to read?

1. Readiness.   Since this is an extension of the discussion in chapter 3 concerning growth marks, let me remind you of my thesis. Not all children mature at the same age. For some unexplained reason, some are ready to read earlier than others. This has absolutely nothing to do with intelligence, parenting, or destiny. It is a matter of fact.

Some children learn to read at a very early age. In fact, there is a heavy dose of material available which suggests that almost all children can learn to read at three. That may be true. Perhaps they can learn to read, but I am not sure I understand why they or their parents want them to. If a child has a natural desire, then he will learn on his own. Otherwise, I see no reason to force a child into reading before he has a social need (school) for the skill.

To affirm this conviction, I made a thorough study of the issue. I asked ten people; but I did select good people. I picked the ten most scholarly people I know—people who read widely and effectively and use their reading as a research tool. I asked each, "At what age did you learn to read?" The reaction was similar for all, men and women alike, "Oh, I don't really remember. It was sometime after I had started the first grade though." This convinced me. If these people could start reading in the first grade and become scholarly, there is no need to force a child into reading at any earlier age.

I do suspect that most children can be forced to read before they are ready, but I also suspect that they will approach the task with something less than intense enthusiasm and will perform according to that level. Perhaps one of the easiest and most effective ways to help a child move into a reading world is to help him develop a readiness for the activity.

Obviously, there is a physical readiness. The child has to be strong enough to hold the book, and he has to be able to focus his eyes on the page. He has to have enough self-control to sit still long enough to get some message from the material. He has to have some understanding that there is a message in the material worth his time and effort to get. He has to be able to remember an image. Some of this can be learned.

Although kindergarten curriculum and aims fluctuate greatly from school to school, most kindergarten programs are designed to move the child toward a readiness for reading. Nevertheless, you still need to assist in the endeavor. There are several things which you can do.

First, and probably most important, read to your child. Start this early and continue it faithfully for as long as you both can still enjoy it. I know families where the father still reads to his family on regular occasions even after the children have reached high school age (and in every case, those are solid families. *I wonder* . . .). From your reading sessions, your child will learn several lessons. He will learn that books carry worthwhile, entertaining messages; he will develop some control of his body; and he will learn that you care about him.

If you have questions about selecting the right material, go see your local librarian. I suggest that anyway. As soon as your child is old enough to walk, take him to the library, get him a card, introduce him to the children's librarian, and request her help in selecting the appropriate material. Librarians are not only trained in such matters, but every one I have met is critically interested in building good reading habits in children. I suspect your librarian will be very happy to help you, and library service is quite reasonable. You can afford that even if you can't afford to buy books.

While you are reading to your child, allow enough time to involve him in the process. Let him look at the pictures first and see if he can anticipate the story. Stop occasionally and show him a particular word. Let him imagine the scene for you. He may even draw it; but whatever you do, make your reading an active process for your child.

If you feel a bit overwhelmed or awkward with all these suggestions, don't worry. I suspect that most parents feel the same way when they first start the endeavor. At least, I did. But we must rely on the child's sense of understanding our intentions. Even if you make all the mistakes in the world, just making an attempt will be significant stimulus in moving your child toward readiness—and it is never too late to start. Even if your child has already grown out of the first three years of school and is already in the fourth or fifth grade, try reading to him anyway. You both may find the sessions quite rewarding.

2. Recognizing the Sounds of Letters.   When I list this as one of the early stages of learning to read, some of the experts will boo and hiss, but some will shout, "Amen!" Although I realize that not all the experts agree on the role of the study of phonics in learning to read, I am convinced. For the past ten years, I have taught college seniors. During that time, I have discovered that those who learned phonics usually have fewer problems in spelling, word formation, and reading than those who didn't. Besides, I am not sure I understand the debate. Learning phonics is a rather simple procedure which surely merits the time your child will spend on it. Since the experts themselves do not agree on its importance, your child's teachers may not be thoroughly convinced, so you may need to be particularly prepared to help your child in this area (provided I have convinced you of its importance).

You can begin by making some flash cards. These don't have to be flashy. In fact the homemade kind may be more interesting. Turn the cereal box inside out and cut it into little squares. Your child may learn to read by studying both sides. When he can pronounce *riboflavin,* he is ready to go on to bigger things.

Make flash cards with letters, with letter combinations, and with words. After you have introduced your child to a sound such as *d,* show him a couple of words that have a *d* sound at the beginning and perhaps at the end. You can still work on the sound as he gets familiar with hearing it in a word. Some of the educational television programs try to make this flash card idea more memorable by giving each sound a personality. If you feel dramatic, you may try techniques such as this.

From the flash cards, you can move into books. Have your child pick out certain letters he recognizes. Very soon he will be pronouncing the words themselves.

You may also want to move him into writing at this stage. While you are still working with the flash cards, you can pronounce the sound and have him write the symbol. This will be the ultimate test of whether he is mastering this particular symbol and sound.

Let me add here that these steps or stages are not necessarily in order. Your child can read and perhaps even read well without a full knowledge of phonics. Don't discourage his reading, but use the phonics study as a supplement.

3. Recognizing the Words.   With a solid background in phonics, your child should be able to develop good skill in deciphering words, including those not in his reading vocabulary. Of course, phonics is not a foolproof method because English words don't always sound as they are supposed to, but it is still a good tool. Again, I would be reluctant to be overly critical of a child's mispronunciation so long as he is being accurate with his phonic reasoning. Learning to read requires taking some risks, so be as positive as possible while the child is still in the beginning stages.

Again, you may want to try the flash cards with words. You can make games out of these. The other day I visited a home where every piece of furniture and ornament was wearing a brightly colored name tag; and when the five-year-old came in, I got a guided tour, not only of the furniture but also of her newly acquired words.

At this stage of your child's development, the most important thing is to have him read to you. But you have to listen and watch closely. He can develop some bad habits here. Watch for such things as transposition—changing the letters around and getting the wrong word. For example, *dog* becomes *god*. Also watch for the potentially bad practice of skipping words. I have known high school students who were particularly hindered by this habit. Make sure your child reads carefully enough to distinguish each letter. Remember the *not* and *now* illustration I used earlier. But the most important thing is to make sure the child is getting the meaning from the context.

Listening to your child read may not be as inviting as watching "M*A*S*H" reruns, but it is absolutely essential at this stage. Learning to read requires some trial and error, taking some risks, and someone has to listen to your child as he goes through this procedure. Although his teacher means well, and I am sure she is doing the best she can, she simply does not have time to listen to every child read as much as he should. If you want your child to read well, you must listen to him during those first three years while he is perfecting the skill and building habits. And once you have started this practice, you just may want to continue it for several years.

4. Reading for Images, Insights, and Meaning.   Even before your child becomes proficient at saying the words, he is also ready to learn that reading is an exciting, entertaining, informative activity. The kind of reader he becomes depends on how well he learns that lesson. If he learns it well, he will have the motivation to read a lot; and as he reads a lot he will become a better reader. There really aren't any shortcuts at this stage. A reader who reads well is one who has read a lot.

Of course, if you took my advice about using the library, you have already begun to teach your child this important lesson. You have shown him that books are valuable. Through your reading to him, you have shown him the entertaining feature of the activity. So you're well on your way; but you still need to encourage him. You can put some importance into his reading. Give him some responsibility. Have him read the road signs when you travel. Have him check the movie ads in the paper to see where the *Star Wars* entry is playing. Make sure he gets some mail, even if you have to bribe someone to write to him. Introduce him to the use of reading as a tool in such things as math, art, and science. Let him read the instructions while you assemble his new bike. (Be careful. Your child and I may be forming a conspiracy.) Make sure his mind is active while he is reading. How do you do that? You discuss his reading with him. This isn't bad dinner table conversation. Make this a common practice. All through his school career, your child will need that kind of interaction with you and with his reading. Not only will you stay in touch with his reading development, you can keep in contact with his whole intellectual and spiritual growth.

Finally, at this stage you need to provide your child with the environment conducive to reading—a comfortable place free from outside stimuli. In other words, you may have to turn off the TV, put the video games in the drawer, and put the Barbies to bed. This may not be as easy as it sounds. Although you may have provided your child with his own room for that very purpose, don't be surprised if he is the kind of person who would rather be with the family. Who wants to go off to an old, cold room to read when all the family warmth and love is somewhere else? So you may have to turn that warmth-and-love room into a reading environment for a while.

5. *Improving Speed.* I am almost reluctant to include this as a stage in reading development because I am not convinced that slow reading is always that much of a liability. Sometimes it may even be an asset. However, some children have some bad habits that can and should be corrected. If the child continues the practice of pronouncing each word, either aloud or silently, he will never achieve a satisfactory speed. Improving this is mostly a matter of reminding and correcting.

After a child learns to read silently, reading speed becomes largely a matter of eye focus—enlarging the space on the page the reader sees at any instant. There are some rather sophisticated machinery and exercises designed to improve eye focus; so if you feel that your child needs to increase his reading speed, you may want to check with his teacher or with a professional reading consultant. Your school district may have such a person on staff.

As I said at the beginning of this chapter, learning to read is a rather mysterious activity that can have a very significant effect on your child's whole intellectual development. If you are a caring parent I urge you to care enough to supervise this process.

As your child becomes proficient in reading, he is ready to do arithmetic, which is the subject of the next chapter.

Chapter 10 at a Glance

1. Good reading habits begin early. Read to your child. Show your child how to build mental images from words.
2. Use your library and children's librarian. Those are valuable services which teach the child that books are important.
3. Many children teach themselves to read. If your preschool child shows signs of wanting to learn, don't discourage him.
4. The skill of reading demands a certain level of maturity. It is often unwise to force a child into it before he has achieved that maturity.
5. Often, the difference between a good reader and a weak reader is a matter of interest. You can help your child develop that interest by showing him what can be gained from reading.
6. Beginning readers need someone to listen to them read!
7. If a beginning reader develops bad habits, these may come back to haunt him.

8. A mastery of phonics may be not necessary to reading but it is still a worthwhile tool which deserves the time it takes to learn.
9. Good readers are people who have read a lot. There aren't many shortcuts.

When I reached the age of five,
Full of joy to be alive,
I opened my mind to fill a lifelong need;
I learned to read.

11

Before Math, During Math, and Aftermath

Just as the experiences of those first three years are so important to the child's reading development, they are also important to his beginning in math skills. Also, since these, like reading, are such personal skills, your child will need a lot of your supervision and cooperation as he becomes proficient in using numbers, recognizing shapes, and solving problems.

In reading, you have to watch your child to see that he doesn't form bad habits. In math, you have to watch to see that he doesn't form bad attitudes. If he forms a bad math habit that hinders his progress, he can usually correct it; but if he gets turned off to math or if he thinks it is beyond him, that attitude can haunt him the rest of his life. To help you be alert to that danger, I present three characteristics of elementary mathematics learning.

Children Between the Ages of Six and Eight Are Concrete Thinkers

At this age, children think about things. They aren't much good at thinking about ideas or theorems or abstractions. If you can remember this while your child is young, you might turn yourself into a fair country math teacher. The principle is simple. Teach your child through things. Teach him to count things. Teach him to add things. Teach him to multiply things. Teach him to divide things. When it comes time for fractions, bake a pie and use it as a model. Show your child the concrete reality of mathematical structure.

I realize that math at its higher level is abstract and theoretical, but at the basic level it simply can't be that way. The child can't handle those abstractions, and to present any kind of numbering principle without showing the child the concrete reality it represents is not only slow and futile, but it can also be discouraging to the child.

Let me assure you that there is a very real psychological phenomenon called math block. I have seen junior high and high school students so frightened by the prospects of mathematics that their whole system runs amok. I am not sure I know all the reasons for that, but I suspect that one of them is that the child was presented abstract math before his mind was ready for it. When your child says, "I don't see," he means it literally, and the way to teach him is to show him something he can see with his eyes. Show him something concrete.

The principle of instruction is simple and easy to apply. For one thing, children want to count and add and multiply things. Put them to work at it. Send the child to the pantry for seven potatoes. Have him count the railroad cars. When you have your child help you count the Christmas cards, use a tally system so your child will get the idea of a nine-base numbering system. As your child becomes proficient with his counting, show him how to count by twos or threes. Use the same principle in teaching him all of the mathematical operations.

Mathematical Operations Are Fundamental to Human Intellect

So you bought him a calculator. Why does he still need to waste so much time drilling on all those facts? I do admit that adding and subtracting and multiplying and solving square roots are machinelike functions sometimes performed better by the machine than by our brains. But these are basic intellectual skills. Most of higher learning is based on these principles. If the child fails to master these basic facts, he will always have intellectual limits. Since so much of our knowledge and so much of our intellectual ability is based on these mathematical facts, the child simply must learn them.

Oh, how I wish there were a creative synonym for that last *learn,* but there isn't. These are facts, rote facts, and the child has to learn them that way; he has to memorize them. We can talk about putting a little variety in the activity, and perhaps even camouflaging it so the child won't know he is learning anything, but it is still memorization and drill. Since these facts are learned through drill, they have to be recited often and with immediate feedback. Consequently, your child's teacher is not going to have enough class time to give your child as much work as he probably needs. So if he is ever going to learn his multiplication tables well enough to keep from getting cheated at the checkout counter, you will have to help him drill. It is just another one of those duties of parenthood.

What method you choose for drilling depends on your personality and patience. If you are into the rapid, straightforward approach, you can use the oral method—problems and answers. But that ignores my first principle that it should be concrete. Flash cards help a little, but it would be even better if you had the child add the flash cards rather than the problems written on them. However, these methods are fast and portable, and your child may find them entertaining. Drill may be more fun than riding in a car or sitting in the doctor's office with nothing to do.

Some games are excellent. A good long game of Monopoly might teach your child about as much math as he will cover in a semester, particularly if you make him the banker. If you don't have games or your child doesn't seem to be interested, make up games that interest him. The only rule is that someone has to keep score. I once watched two second graders play the hand-slap game for about an hour. It is actually rather simple and portable. The person who's "it" holds his hands upside down at waist level. The other person rests his hands on top. "It" jerks one or both of his hands out and slaps the other person's hands before he can move. These two second graders had worked out a point system, so that they were practicing their arithmetic while entertaining themselves on a stalled school bus. Try something like that with your child. It might be fun for the two of you to invent a math-learning game. You can both play enthusiastically.

I also encourage you to give the child some responsibility to use his math skills in a practical way. Of course, you have to adjust the problem to his skill level, but you can give him a feeling of the importance of this information he has been storing in his brain. For example, try this, "I need a gallon of milk at $1.89 and a loaf of bread at $.66. Will I have enough left out of my $5.00 to buy you that box of crayons?" That ought to start the brain clicking. With a problem like this, he will not only practice his rote skills of computation, he will also begin to use higher-level problem-solving skills. Use every opportunity you get to engage your child in this kind of activity. When it is convenient, have him solve problems of measurement, time, and percentage. This way, he will become familiar with particular kinds of solutions. Have him figure the baby-sitter's fee. If he is interested in sports, introduce him to the wonderful world of batting averages or field goal percentages.

Math problems are all around us. With just a little imagination, you can bring the real world into your child's learning so that he will not only have the concrete representation, but he can also see the purpose for all that rote drill.

Math Is Not Exclusive to the Male Mentality!

I am not trying to get into trouble here; I am trying to avoid it. Statistics tend to indicate that mathematics is a male-dominated field. There are more males than females in the higher-level math courses in high school and college. More men than women enter the math-related fields. (That makes sense, given the first statistic.) But this is a cultural phenomenon rather than a natural one. There is nothing inherent in the study of mathematics that says your ninth-grade daughter should have a natural block against learning algebra. If she has such a block, she learned it.

Through the years, I have become convinced that math interest and ability is largely the result of early training and association. For example, at our college this year we will produce three very fine female math teachers. One is a farmer's daughter who had to count cows and measure the corn when she was young. Another is the daughter of an architect whose home is filled with math games and erector sets. The third is a daughter of a math teacher. I rest my case.

If you don't want your daughter to fall in among the bad attitudes toward math, surround her with the reality of concrete mathematical problems and encourage her as she grows. And that is also good advice when dealing with your son.

Like reading, mathematical operations are learned skills. With the proper stimuli, circumstances, supervision and encouragement, your child can become proficient enough at those skills to achieve his created potential. But he also needs to learn to write, which is the subject of the next chapter.

Chapter 11 at a Glance

1. Arithmetic tables are fundamental to human knowledge. They are learned through drill—repetition and feedback.

2. At its simplest level, mathematics is a concrete activity dealing with concrete things. Early lessons in math should employ this concreteness.
3. Math block (the inability to succeed at math) is an attitude and not a curse of creation. It can be prevented and corrected.
4. Play family games that require math operations.
5. Give the child chores and responsibilities that show your confidence in his math skills.

12
Writing to Become Exact

When a child enters the first grade, he barely knows how to hold a pencil while he draws his name. When he comes out of the third grade we expect him to be an accomplished author. That is a big chunk of growth and development to be crowded into three short years. Like reading and arithmetic, writing is a learned, personal skill that requires individual supervision and direction.

If you want your child to develop the right skills and attitudes toward the two dimensions of writing—penmanship and expression—you will have to assist the teacher. She simply does not have enough time to provide every child with sufficient encouragement and feedback. But to be of greatest assistance to your child, you need to understand both the writing process and your own child's special level of maturity. To get a better idea of what your child is going to experience, let's study those two dimensions as separate skills.

Penmanship

Most children make rather rapid progress in the simple skill of making intelligent marks on paper. They have to. We expect rapid progress in this area. We expect them to go from the fundamentals of pencil holding through primitive drawing into cursive writing in three years. To start with, penmanship is not all that natural as a skill. There is probably no other physical activity quite like the activity of holding a pencil and making it operate the way we want it to. When the child first reaches the age when he begins writing, he has probably not had any previous experience that will help him master the art. The act of writing requires the child to use a new set of muscles in a different way. Frequently, five- and six-year-old children simply don't have the muscular maturity to hold the pencil the way we would like them to hold it; so those children learn to compensate. To see how original children can be in learning to compensate for their muscular immaturity at that stage, visit my class of college seniors and look at all the varieties of pencil holding and letter construction among those young adults, all still practicing skills they learned during their first three years of school.

Although the penmanship experts disagree about the correct way to hold a pencil and they disagree about what to do with the child who manages incorrectness, the general feeling is that if the child is succeeding at his unique style, we should leave him alone.

Of course, there are some specific ways to help him. First, get your child an oversized pencil. Most of his physical activity up to this point has been big-muscle movement. Writing requires small- and precise-muscle control. At this stage, a fat pencil is easier to grasp and direct. As the child improves his small-muscle control, he will soon grow out of his need for that oversized pencil, and you can move him to the regular size. In fact, you can make a reward out of this. Order him a pencil from Disneyland or some other exotic place, and present it to him when he masters the skill of pencil control. That should bribe him into practicing.

When the child is first learning the art of holding and directing the pencil, don't discourage his spontaneous creations. Let him practice controlling the pencil to make what he wants to make. Don't put too many limits on him by insisting that he write his name or something significant. Any practice in pencil control is valuable. If your child likes to imitate, draw a page full of designs for him—circles, diagonal lines, letters, numbers—and let him control the pencil. Encourage him to draw pictures.

If your child needs help to get the pencil to go where it is supposed to in making the correct symbols (such as letters or numbers), buy him a set of letter blocks and have him practice by tracing his finger through the letters. Also, you can stand behind him as he is sitting at his desk, put your finger in the middle of his back, and trace a letter. This will usually transfer over into his hand. This technique is particularly valuable if your child is getting some little part of a letter wrong such as putting the hump on the wrong side of the letter *p*. Incidentally, I first encountered these two techniques while reading the educational theories of Quintilian, a first-century Roman. Obviously, children and penmanship have not changed all that much in the last two thousand years.

Another valuable technique is for you to break the task of writing down into manageable parts. If you show your child the number 5, he may get overwhelmed with the size of the task. But if you show him a straight line across, a straight line down, and a little curl on the bottom, he should be able to imitate that. Actually, this is an important teaching theory for any study at any age. If we tell ourselves that we can't learn something, we are usually overwhelmed with the total picture. If someone breaks it down into manageable parts for us, we can learn those parts, put them together, and master the task. To prove that, I, a world-class klutz, learned to juggle the other day. Imagine that! This guy who keeps daily records by soup stains on his tie instead of a diary, juggles. It is actually rather simple—just a series of individual hand movements that can be learned one by one. Do your child a favor. Break his penmanship task down into distinct, manageable hand movements.

If you are committed to helping your child practice during that special time when he is learning to print his letters, please check with his teacher. There are so many different styles of printing lurking around first-grade classes that you will need to know what and how he is being taught at school. Many of these more recent styles of printing are designed to look like cursive so that the child will not have as much difficulty making the transition from printing.

Since penmanship is a physical skill, the key to learning and improving is the same as in any other physical skill—practice. Although some children may seem to be more natural because they are better coordinated at the small-muscle movement, almost all children can learn to write legibly with enough practice and feedback. To make the practice palatable, give the child some practical, real chores that require him to write. Encourage him to practice his penmanship through his desire to express himself.

Expression

Although learning to hold a pencil and make intelligible marks on paper may not be a natural skill, it is worth learning because we need to express ourselves. We need some means to say what we think. We need some way to share our feelings and ideas. We need some method for convincing and persuading other people of our position when we know we are right.

If you can convince your child of the value of writing as a means of expression, you will probably produce a good writer, competent both in penmanship skills as well as the skills of written expression. Actually, competent expression is more of an attitude anyway. Good writing grows out of confidence. If the person is confident that he has something worthwhile to communicate, he will almost always find the means to express himself.

From the very beginning, the child should be convinced that he is learning these skills so he can share his ideas with a wider audience. In fact, it is rather common and perhaps healthy for the more confident children to become frustrated with their written language skills at the early stages. They really want to say more than they have the tools to say. One of the tests to see whether you have done a good job of creating a positive attitude toward writing is to count how many times your child bothers you to spell words for him. Usually, this is a good sign for a first, second, or third grader. It indicates that he understands the value of the written language. Whatever you do about all the pestering, don't discourage that attitude. It will be valuable to him throughout his school career.

But how do you foster that attitude? Although some of it may be natural,—just the way this particular child is—some of it can be developed; and this is what you can influence.

You can begin early, about as soon as the child becomes competent in oral language. Have him dictate to you—a story, a poem, a letter to Grandmother—while you write it for him. Show him his work. Have him read it himself, often. Let him see what he has created. Remind him of the time when he will be old enough to eliminate the steno. Make this a regular practice, and keep it going well into his school career. As he becomes competent in writing, he can be the steno while both of you dictate. Teach the child not to be afraid of his own mind.

When he finally learns to write, read what he has written. Writing is a form of expression. The very definition suggests that somebody read and interact with what we have written. When I put the finishing touches on this chapter, I plan to put on my boots, wade a mile through fourteen inches of snow to my wife's office and demand that she read it. I want feedback and I want it now. And besides, I know she will be sensitive, even if she doesn't agree with everything I have said. Although your seven-year-old may not be as childish as I am, he still appreciates your interest in what he has written. If you show interest, he will write more. Again, since teachers are busy, they may not always have enough time to provide your child with as much feedback as his writing deserves. Just to make sure, assign yourself the task.

Make some games out of your child's writing skills. Your second grader is probably capable of publishing a family newspaper, but you may have to give him the idea. A production of an original musical comedy played in the backyard for all the local dogs and neighbors would not only fill a summer afternoon, but would also provide an opportunity for your child to exercise some writing skills.

Such activities in written expression can teach your child several valuable lessons. Through these, he can develop a sense of confidence, and this confidence will help him develop his creativity and imagination. Since writing demands sense awareness, the child will learn to be more astute as a listener and observer. Sometimes simple drills in listing sense feedback is an excellent writing activity. Take your child to the park. When you get home, have him make a list of the sounds and smells and sights he remembers. Single words in a straight line are sufficient. He will learn the lesson of expression.

Writing is also an excellent activity to teach the skill of organization—of organizing thoughts and images and ideas so that they can be filed in the mind for future use or they can be communicated in an orderly fashion. The skill of organization is one of the most valuable skills a person can master. If you can help your child develop it, you will have performed a great service. You can begin this even back in those prewriting days when the child is still dictating his stories to you. Encourage him to observe in some kind of order. Have him send a description of his room to his grandmother, but make him see it in order. When he tells you a story, help him get the events in chronological order. If he has an idea, help him put it into an outline. Incidentally, that skill of organization will ultimately lead to the skill of outlining, and outlining is a must for any effective, productive writer or speaker.

Written expression not only demands basic knowledge of the language, but it also teaches the language. The best way to teach such things as vocabulary, spelling, or sentence construction is to have the child write. Be prepared to answer his questions. Be prepared to make suggestions for improvement. (Regardless of what some language experts tell us, I still feel that a word spelled correctly communicates more than a misspelled word.) If you are not totally confident in your own ability in punctuation, capitalization, or other points of usage, invest in a good grammar handbook. *The Plain English Handbook,* written by the Walshes and published by Random House-McCormick-Mathers still sells for less than five dollars; and it lists all the rules in a neat order so that you can get to them quickly.

As I said at the beginning of this chapter, good writing is more of an attitude than a skill. If your child has enough confidence in himself that he wants to share his ideas, he will probably learn the skills needed to achieve his goals.

In the past three chapters, I have focused on three basic skills of learning and intellect. During his first three years in school, your child will make tremendous strides in mastering these skills and moving toward becoming an intellectually independent person. If you pause to reflect about what is happening to your child, you will become almost overwhelmed with the rapid change.

Such an abrupt increase in intellectual powers brings with it a whole new slate of curiosities, needs, and demands. Since the intellect must always seek its direction and approval from the spiritual, we turn now to that part of your child.

Chapter 12 at a Glance

1. Pencil control requires small-muscle control. It is a matter of physical growth.

2. Writing requires the confidence to put our thoughts on paper. You can help your child learn to write by encouraging him to communicate through the written word.

3. At this stage, the child's speaking vocabulary may be much larger than his writing vocabulary. He may get discouraged because he can't spell the words he wants to use. Help him avoid that discouragement. Spell the words for him. At this point, he needs to express himself.

4. If your child asks you to read what he has written, read it. Give him immediate feedback.

5. Encourage your child to tell stories, jokes, and so on. He will get the sense of chronology, structure, coherence, and language flow.

13

The Spiritual Matters

As your child develops his skills of reading, writing, and mastering mathematics, he will become more aware of himself and his environment, and he will begin to ask questions about his role in that environment. He may not always know that he is asking those questions, but he is; and that curiosity is spiritual in its character. Although I don't intend to anticipate the Holy Spirit here and say that every child automatically pauses somewhere in the middle of the second grade and analyzes his relationship with God, a growing knowledge does lead the child to a need for more answers.

Whether your child has made a profession of faith or not, you must realize his specific needs for instruction and direction during this critical period when his knowledge level is expanding so rapidly. Usually his spoken or subconscious spiritual questions can be classified into three types: knowledge of God and Christ, the nature of faith, and applied values.

In this brief chapter, I will not attempt to anticipate nor to answer all the questions, but only suggest a framework for you to use in understanding what is happening to your child. There are some very intelligent people who have devoted their lives to understanding the spiritual needs of young children. I recommend that you spend some time becoming familiar with their ideas and insights. You can find their books at your local bookstore.

Knowledge of God and Christ

Perhaps the most important thing for you to remember about your child at this age is that he is a concrete thinker. He is simply more comfortable thinking about things he can see and hear. The magnificent, eternal, omnipresent character of God may baffle him. In fact, one rogue, Jean Jacques Rousseau, once said that any child who believes in God is an idolator. I think Rousseau was wrong because he underestimated the capacity of children, but we do need to realize the danger. During this time when the child is beginning to use his mental powers to interpret the written codes of culture, we need to present a God he can know concretely, the God of creation. The changing of the seasons, birds flying South in winter, the swallows returning to Capistrano, the individual fingerprints, the beauty of a tree, the four-o'clock which closes its blossoms in the daytime, all proclaim coherence, order, and unity. Make your devotions from these things and your child will soon begin to see the Mind that has made them.

Since the child is developing his ability to read, now is the time to stimulate his interest in discovering God's Word. If he can't read well enough to handle the actual Scripture, find him a good Bible storybook. If your library doesn't have those, drop into your church library or a Christian bookstore. There are several good ones available.

You can also supplement the Bible storybooks with other kinds of children's books written from a Christian perspective. Any story that teaches the child the nature and character of God or introduces him to the well-known stories in Scripture is a valuable experience at this stage, particularly if the story is written so the child can read it himself and stay interested in it. Such reading will help build some anticipation for reading the Bible, and it will give him a background for grasping the Scripture when he gets to it. This is important because through the years, I have talked with several beginning readers who have developed an unhealthy fear of the Bible because of the way it was treated in sermons or Sunday school classes or even in the home. One of the difficult characteristics about rearing a prereader is that we are never quite sure what they hear and how they interpret what they hear. You can guard against your child's inadvertently developing a fear of Scripture by providing him with exciting devotional reading. Just recently, I saw the results of a poll of librarians who had named C. S. Lewis's *The Lion, the Witch, and the Wardrobe* as one of the top ten children's books of all times. That is quite a recommendation, particularly from a group that is not necessarily Christian. Again, visit your library or bookstore. There is an ample supply of solid, well-written material the child can read on his own in his search for understanding God and God's place in his life.

At the same time though, don't give him the total responsibility to find out on his own. Now is the time to involve the child actively in family devotions. If your family has not been having regular group devotions, you may want to start during this time when your child is moving from a nonreading into a reading world. The group devotion is probably more important at this point than at any other stage in the child's development. The child is being introduced to such a variety of topics, issues, and values that he needs some framework for basing his questions so he can handle all that new information. Provide him with that structure. You don't have to be a theologian or a great preacher. Read, pray, and listen to the child's questions and ideas. He will understand if you have to search for answers. But through all this he should get the idea that his spiritual life matters to you and to him.

The Nature of Faith

Christian parents frequently ask me, "At what age is a child old enough to hear and understand the message of salvation so that he can make a profession of faith?" My answer is probably too simple—"When he asks." But I am willing to live with that answer as a general principle. When your child comes to you with questions that indicate he is concerned about death, heaven, hell, or his own relationship with Christ, he is ready to have those questions answered succinctly and simply. He doesn't need tons of sermons. He doesn't need to study the four spiritual laws. He needs to know that Christ worked out the plan of salvation on the cross and in resurrection; and the child needs to know that he can have a personal relationship with his eternal Savior through faith and prayer. This may seem like an oversimplification of all the mysteries of theology, but Christ taught us that faith is simple. Let the child understand simply. As he grows intellectually, his understanding will grow. If your child is old enough to ask, he is old enough to believe.

If you don't feel comfortable answering his questions yourself, you may want to seek some outside help; but be careful about whom you choose for that help. This is a special time for your child. These are very personal questions he is asking. Unless your child is particularly bold and outspoken, it probably took a lot of courage just for him to ask you. Help him guard the personal, private character of his search for a meaningful relationship with God. If your child knows the pastor personally, the pastor can help; but if the pastor doesn't know your child, the pastor is a wrong choice. Pick someone who has at least had a conversation with your child before this time.

On occasions, I have been asked to meet with children I don't know. Inevitably, the situation becomes embarrassing for the child, for the parents, and for me. I consider myself fairly effective in talking with children. (Having a twelve-year-old mind is of some advantage.) But I am never good in these sessions. Regardless of my jovial nature, the child simply doesn't know me well enough to share those personal, profound thoughts that have been flashing across his mind. These are things you only share with someone who loves you.

But what if your child never comes to you with the questions or doesn't even hint that he has the questions? How long do you wait for him to make the move? Is there something a parent can do to lead the child toward readiness for faith? Yes, obviously. After you have provided your child with reading materials, church opportunities, and at least some family devotional sessions, you may want to encourage him to ask his questions by asking him some questions. Look for the proper opportunity, some time when you and your child are feeling good about being related to each other, when you are both happy and honest, and ask him what he thinks about Christ, what are the advantages of being a Christian, and what he thinks about the value of prayer. If he is reluctant to talk about those things, answer your questions yourself; then drop the matter. In a few weeks when another opportunity presents itself, come back to the same questions.

There are, however, a couple of notes of caution. Although I realize that the Christian message is victory over death, I would be cautious about overemphasizing the death theme with a child of this age. It is quite possible that this theme could so completely dominate his mind that he loses sight of the real theme of victory.

The early Puritans didn't have any reservations about this. Their children's literature is laced with the idea of death. *The New England Primer,* a popular primary textbook in colonial America, taught the child the letter *X* by having him recite this verse: "Xerses the Great did die, and so must you and I," but it also taught the child the letter *F* by having him recite: "The idle Fool is whipped at school." I am not convinced that children need to dwell on the idea of death before they are fully prepared to handle the perplexity.

The second note of caution is that you make sure the climate is right. Since you are seeking to enter the child's most inner being, don't do it in a moment of anger which would only make the child defensive. On occasions, both as a parent and a teacher, I have felt like yelling, "You stupid jerk. You are going to hell if you don't change your heart and ways." But that probably isn't the right thing to say, particularly at that moment. Wait for a time when your child is not defensive or trembling. Wait for the moment when both of you can be honest.

I repeat an earlier statement. If your child is old enough to ask, he is old enough to hear the message and make a decision. If he doesn't ask, you may want to prompt him.

Applied Values

When I first planned this section of the book, I was going to make value development into a chapter by itself; but that wouldn't be in keeping with my idea of values. I realize that there are values apart from religion. I realize that nonbelievers are capable of building a structure of valuing that can be as specific and noble as mine which flows from a personal commitment to living a God-centered life. But the difference is that the Christian's value structure has a base. He knows the source of the instruction that directs his beliefs and his behavior. Regardless of situations, his basic commitment cannot change. It just seems appropriate that a discussion of your child's value development should be included in the discussion of his spiritual development.

These first few years in school are critical. For one thing, when the child starts school, he simply doesn't spend as much time with you. He has more opportunity to make and act on his own decisions. Since he is growing in independence and self-control, he will now confront issues that have never really been an issue before. He has to take charge of at least some areas of his own life.

This first taste of the power of decision making comes at a time when the child is not all that reasonable. He has not yet developed the ability to reason through actions and see the long-range consequences. He has to limit his thoughts to what a decision is going to mean to him at the moment. At this stage, the key to his value decisions may be acceptance and approval. If he wants to please you and win your approval, he will probably do what he thinks it will take to please you. However, as his social circles broaden, don't be surprised if he decides he would rather win some other person's approval (such as a playmate who encourages him to play with matches or throw snowballs at cars).

As the child grows in independence, moral decisions become more difficult. The difference between right and wrong becomes less clear than it once was.

In order to sort through things, most children try trial and error. They decide (perhaps not consciously) to experiment with behaviors to see how they like them. The problem for the parent is to keep from panicking. How often a distraught parent has called me with the shameful confession, "My seven-year-old has lied to me." For some reason, that first lie is a real shocker. I remember the first time each of my children lied to me. I was heartbroken, beside myself, and I made a vow never to admit it to anyone. Now, fifteen years later, I am amused at how I responded, not only to the lie but to a lot of experimental behavior during that time when the child was first adjusting to the new social and moral demands of school. If your child is to develop any kind of moral self-control, he has to experiment; and you can keep your sanity by telling yourself, *Maybe it won't look all this bad twenty years from now.*

But you can—you must—provide the base and the feedback. Trial and error is not all that bad as a learning technique if the child knows what he should do and he knows when he gets out of line. Be prepared to tell him. Don't confuse your child by reserving your judgment about his behavior. If you are really disturbed, make the message emphatic enough that the child will remember your displeasure the next time he encounters the same opportunity. That emphatic message is called punishment, but we will get back to that later.

Make sure your child knows what you value. There are two ways to communicate this—tell him and show him. Use those devotional sessions to teach the child what the Bible says about taking care of his body and managing social relationships. When your child is at this stage of intellectual and moral development, you can be matter-of-fact and specific. "I do this because this is what God's Word tells me to do." I realize that this sounds authoritarian, but at this age the child will respond to authority. Rejoice for now. When he gets to junior high, that approach won't work anymore. He will bug you for the reason behind every decision you or God ever made.

This authoritarian base becomes a bench mark. The child may be disobedient, but he knows that he is being disobedient. He has to make a choice to disobey. Without this base, he only confuses himself, and his trial-and-error approach runs on endlessly. Besides, we have the promise of Scripture itself that this kind of instruction will be blessed by God as the child grows.

To show you what kind of an old traditionalist I am, I still believe in having the child memorize some Bible verses. It definitely won't hurt him. Memorizing is good mind skill, and it might be invaluable. When my child comes to the place where he has to make a decision about using drugs (and almost every child growing up in this country will eventually face that decision), I want him to remember Paul's admonition about his body being a temple of the Holy Spirit. That may not deter my child, but it will make him know that what he is doing is wrong. I want the biblical value structure planted firmly in his mind.

When your child makes a decision to transgress his basic value structure, you need to remind him. How you choose to remind him should depend on what your child needs rather than how angry you are at the moment. In other words, if you have to punish your child, remember *why* you are punishing him. You are not trying to prove that you are bigger than he is; he knows that already. You are not trying to show that you have been hurt or wronged. You are trying to show your child that he has made an inaccurate moral choice, and you are trying to remind him not to do it again. Effective punishment gets that message across. You may need to be creative. The standard "belt to the seat" may not always be the best way to convey that idea. Personally, I have always found the most painful punishment for a mistake is to have to make restitution. But whatever punishment or reminder you choose, let the child make full restitution. When the punishment is complete, forget the crime. Go right back to your relationship as if nothing ever happened. This ability to forget and return to normal is not always easy, but it is vital.

As your child develops his intellectual tools of reading, writing, and problem solving, he will develop a spiritual awareness. And this spiritual awareness comes at a time when his expanding social contacts put him into the position of making significant moral decisions. In an almost contradictory manner, as the child grows in school, his need for solid, parental instruction increases. Children are fun at any age, but they are particularly fun at this age when they need us the most.

Chapter 13 at a Glance

1. Just as the time between six and eight is a period of rapid physical and mental growth, it is also a period of rapid growth in

spiritual awareness. Children should hear the truth of Christ in straightforward, simple language.

2. Spiritual matters are very personal; thus, parents should be the primary source of instruction for children of this age.

3. If your family does not have regular devotions, you may want to start them during the time your child is starting to school. Family worship time is important for several reasons.

4. Since children develop moral decision-making processes through trial and error, they need a solid, authoritarian base (the Bible) as a touchstone.

5. There is a difference between children who know the difference between right and wrong and choose to do wrong and those children who don't know the difference.

14

The Changing Role of Television

Speaking of morals, how do you feel about television? It would be rather easy for me to go into a long tirade here, warning you about that demon monster we have allowed into our houses. I could tell you about the research which shows that children learn aggressiveness and even violence from TV. I could talk about the absurd programming which brings into our living rooms sights and suggestions that weren't fit fare for even an adult twenty years ago. Or I could simply relate the information that the average American school child spends about six hours per day in front of the TV. That is one-fourth of his life.

But I am going to resist the urge to remind you of these things because television is a reality. Whether we like the box or the programming, we are still living in a television society. Your child will live all his life in the company of TV.

That isn't all bad. The concept of television is a good learning idea. In most learning situations, we employ only one sense. We either hear something or we see something. In television, we see and hear at the same time, so the potential for our learning is vastly increased—more than doubled. But this makes the programming even more significant. Since television is such an effective teaching tool, we need to be cautious about what we allow ourselves and our children to learn from it. We really don't solve any problems by denying the existence of television. We are postponing them. Television is here to stay, and it has the potential of being an effective teaching instrument in our society. We now need to learn how to use it, and we need to teach our children how to use it. Unfortunately not enough of us have mastered that lesson yet.

The appropriate time to begin that study, if you have not already, is when the child begins his journey into school and reading. Both these intellectual and social activities heighten his awareness. As his vocabulary and attention span develop, he will simply receive more stimuli from a television program. He will hear more words, see more scenes, and respond to more situations. As he develops the ability to organize, he will retain more of what he has seen. As he learns to interact with what he is reading, his emotional response to television will increase. In simple terms, watching TV is a different activity for a reader than for a nonreader. If you have a TV in your home, you need to be aware of this transition because your child is going to need some instruction and supervision.

For one thing, your child will soon be able to distinguish between reality and fantasy. At that time, he will need some help in dealing with emotions during programs that are most realistic. He may be able to recognize the bloody, unreal detective shows as so much imagination, which can be passed off easily, but a program such as the old "Little House on the Prairie" may make a deep impression. Since television is such a powerful tool, his emotions during such real-life drama could become quite intense. If he watches such drama you will have to watch with him. You will have to offer him counsel and encouragement.

Let me illustrate. One Saturday afternoon, my wife and I watched an old Western movie. In the space of two hours we saw about fourteen guys get blown away in some kind of violence or another. At the end of the movie, we watched about fifteen minutes of a live sports program. A high diver hit the water incorrectly and lay at the bottom of the pool until the rescuers could pull him up. We were almost in a state of shock as we sat glued to our seats, watching this drama unfold before our eyes.

We had just watched fourteen guys get blown away in fictional death, but the possibility of real death disturbed us greatly. Because the scene was too personal and demanded too much emotion, I almost wished I weren't watching; but I couldn't bring myself to the point of actually turning off the set. Through this medium of television, I was trapped. I found comfort in having my wife present so we could talk about the event as it happened, and we have discussed it occasionally in the weeks that followed. Obviously, both of us still remember it. The picture was too real for us to forget the moment.

Television has the power of bringing that same kind of experience to your child. How he needs someone with him when that moment comes! Study carefully what you let him watch by himself. Not only does he need you to help him through the moral problems some programs present, but he may need you to help him manage the emotional problems that arise out of the programs which are closer to his reality.

Another problem that comes from a constant diet of television watching is that it teaches the child to turn outside stimuli—visual and aural—off and on at will. This ability isn't much of an asset when the teacher is trying to tell the class the events leading to the Revolutionary War. But I can understand how the child develops the skill. Living in a room with a constant flow of pictures and sounds—some interesting and some not so interesting—can really foul up our ability to concentrate. The solution to this may be rather simple: Turn the set off occasionally. I am not opposed to letting children watch a given program. In fact, frequently a good television program will inspire a child to read or to think or even to create. But we cannot allow TV to become an opium which lulls us into states of semiconsciousness. To control this, use the on-and-off switch. If there is a program you and your child want to watch, watch it. But when it is over, turn the set off. Fill the room with silence and imagination. Eliminate that thing which is demanding semi-attention so that you can concentrate fully on the reality at hand.

Actually, this idea isn't original with me. I learned it in a teaching book which warned me about leaving the overhead projector on after it had served its usefulness to the class. We can just receive so many stimuli at a given time. It we get too many, we lose our ability to concentrate. Any generation raised on a television diet is susceptible to this malady.

Television also permits the child to be passive mentally. Why do we need to draw mental images when someone will draw them for us? But drawing mental images is basic to our intellect. Between the ages of six and eight, the child learns to create, formulate, and plan through the exercise of drawing mental pictures, either from what he is reading or from what he makes up himself. If he begins to rely too heavily on television, he could lose the thrill of making his own pictures.

You can prevent this by making sure your child has ample opportunity to read and to imagine. You may want to use his favorite TV show as a starting point. Have him write the next show. If he can't write yet, let him dictate the show to you and you write it for him. Have him put the characters in unusual places, meeting unusual people. Activate your child in language activities. Make sure he is speaking, writing, and reading. Too much absorbing will only make him intellectually, and perhaps physically, flabby.

This leads us to the next point. Between the ages of six and eight, your child will grow intellectually and spiritually, but he is also going to grow physically. During this time he needs lots of exercise. What he gets at school in recess or P.E. is simply not enough. Of course, if your child is active and creative, you may get the idea that he gets too much exercise; but if he is a passive child, he could rely on the television as an excuse for not getting the exercise his developing body needs.

Just turning off the set may not be sufficient in this case. You may have to learn to play yourself, or you may need to introduce him to activities outside the home and school. In fact, that is the subject of the next chapter.

Chapter 14 at a Glance

1. Television is a good educational tool when used correctly.
2. When the child is playing or reading, turn the set off. Don't use it as a background for play.
3. Television programs deserve discussion. Watch with your child so you can discuss with him.
4. As the child grows more literate, his ability to comprehend the subtleties of a television program increases.

15

Outside Activities

When the child starts school, the family usually is faced with another decision. How involved is this child going to be in those activities outside the home and the school which are so popular across the nation? This is more than the child's question. It is one the whole family must answer because the child's participation will require some kind of commitment from all family members. Such participation directs time schedules, causes transportation problems, and requires your active encouragement and perhaps instruction in another phase of the child's growth. Is the activity worth the effort?

To answer this, you need to assess the actual value of the participation to both the child and the family. To facilitate your evaluation, we can classify these outside activities into three groups: participation activities, instructional activities, and clubs.

Participation Activities

In this category, I include organized sports teams and musical and drama groups. Although there is some instruction inherent in the very nature of these activities, the groups are primarily for the purpose of giving the child the social structure for participation.

The directing principle determining your child's involvement is an honest answer to a simple question: Why do you want your child to participate? Does he have the desire? Do you think it will be educational? Or are you interested in fulfilling some of your own aspirations through your child? One of those answers is correct; one is incorrect; and one is probably the result of wishful thinking.

If your child really wants to join a sports team (baseball, football, soccer, wrestling, or hockey seem to be the most popular) or an orchestra when he is six, seven, or eight years old, he may be mature enough to handle the experience. Some children are and some aren't, and there is nothing sadder than to watch a seven-year-olds' baseball game where four mature athletes dominate the contest at the expense of all players involved. I wouldn't propose to take this experience away from those who are ready for it, but I see no need to force a child into such an experience when he is neither physically nor emotionally mature enough to enjoy some success. If your child is interested, he may be ready.

On the other hand, if you have great visions of being the parent of the world's first eight-year-old all-American quarterback you need to look somewhere else to fulfill your fantasies. Being eight years old is tough enough in itself. Your child doesn't need the added burden of carrying you on his back. Don't force your child into any activity in which he has to carry your standard of success. That is unfair to the child. If he does choose to play, help him set realistic standards for himself. Even the pros boot a ground ball or blow a wrong note.

If your child is talented and mature enough to master the skill of the activity, the whole experience can be quite educational for him. He can learn how to function in a group; he can learn how to deal with success and failure; and through participation he will surely develop his skills in the activity. But the question is at what age we need to start him so that he will learn the valuable lessons without first learning that he doesn't like the activity.

Frequently I meet parents who tell me that they suspect their child is talented. They don't want to cheat him out of the opportunity to be as good as he can be. I agree with them. We should give our children every chance to achieve their created potential;

but as a college football coach, I am convinced that it is not necessary to start a child into sports before his body and emotions are mature enough to handle the rigors and discipline of the sport. We have fine college players who never participated in organized sports, much less football, until they were in high school. We even have a few players who started football after they were in college. Usually these young men bring a refreshing eagerness to the game which the early starters have lost somewhere in the many seasons they have played.

The above paragraph was written from the sports perspective, but my music consultants tell me the same is true with band and orchestra. Enthusiasm for practice and playing is more important than early experience.

Of course, the greatest value of participation is that your child will get the exercise and socialization he needs; so if you and he choose not to participate, you will have to provide him with some other opportunity to keep his body active.

If he does participate in such organized events, he will still need a great deal of attention and supervision; so your role is just beginning. For one thing, he will need individual instruction and practice in the activity. Playing a horn or throwing a baseball is a physical skill. To master it, your child will have to practice it. If he has any ability at all, the more he practices, the better he will get. But practice in the individual skills is a one-on-one activity. Just as the teacher does not have enough time to give your child's reading as much attention as it needs, the coach is not going to have enough time to teach him how to catch or throw a baseball. If you want him to become proficient at these skills, you have to play catch with him. Hour by hour you have to play catch with him. If you agree to let your child participate in organized baseball, it is only fair that you take on this responsibility of helping him develop his skills. It simply isn't fair to let him be embarrassed after the game starts.

You will need to help the child manage the authorities such as the orchestra leader or the coach. Sometimes the people supervising these activities are quite effective at what they do, but some know more about the activity than they know about children. In all my years in sports, the worst tirades and the most unreasonable demands I have ever heard have come not from pro, college, or high school coaches, but they have come from coaches in the youth programs. If your child draws one of the sensitive, effective coaches or directors, rejoice. If he gets one of the other kind, consider again why the child is in the activity.

As one final caution, I will say frankly that I am opposed to any activity which alters a child's natural growth in the interest of his sports success. If the child is active and is eating a balanced diet, I am opposed to his starving some weight off just to get into the wrestling class. If the child is active and in reasonable condition, I am opposed to putting him on a weight-lifting program just to pump up his muscles for a football season. Those are activities for adults who have already settled into a body type, but developing children need room to grow naturally.

If you do decide that your child should participate in either a sports, music, or drama program and you don't know where to find one, contact the school. Frequently these programs identify, at least loosely, with the school. If the school people can't help you, try your local community newspapers.

Of course, if you and your child do choose for him to participate in an organized program, you will need to adjust the family schedule to accommodate his commitment. But you know that already, so we will get on to the next kind of activity.

Instructional Activities

Some parents and children choose programs in which instruction is the primary objective. These include such things as dance classes, gymnastic classes, music lessons, or swimming lessons. If you do a bit of research and select the right school, it is possible that your child will get excellent instruction from qualified instructors who understand both the activity and children. Because the supervisor is not responsible for so many children and because the public performance is not as important as in the participation activities, your child should get more individual attention and supervision.

Although your child may miss the lessons of teamwork those other activities provide, he will receive more actual instruction and practice in the skill itself.

If your child shows an interest and an aptitude for one of these instructional activities and you are prepared to make the time and financial commitment to it, I would encourage you to choose the school as carefully as you choose a doctor. Get personal testimony from satisfied customers. Any parent who has been paying for piano lessons will take a few minutes to give you her impression of the teacher. Check out the facilities. If you choose an activity such as gymnastics which demands huge space and a large investment for equipment, don't be so critical of the actual structure; but look for such things as safety and cleanliness. Meet the instructors. I repeat myself. Meet the instructors. And soon after your child has started the activity, drop in unexpectedly and watch the lesson in progress.

For you, these lessons represent an investment of time, money, and your own flesh and blood. You are entitled to see what you are paying for. As I said in the chapter about schools, the key to any learning situation is the instructor. A creative instructor who can relate to your child is far more important than the equipment and the facilities.

Another advantage of these schools or classes is that these instructors are usually professional enough to recognize special talent. If your child is particularly gifted, the instructor may be able to spot that talent early, and the school may be able to offer you some advice about how to nurture the talent without destroying your child's wholesomeness. Of course, there is always a word of warning. Don't mistake early maturity for natural talent. Children do change in body style and attitude as they develop. If your child shows unusual ability for his age, encourage him, but prepare both yourself and him for the possibility that his teammates may catch up in a few years.

Of course, these instructional activities do require a financial commitment, so you will always have to consider the cost against the gain. There are times when such programs might not be feasible regardless of your economic status, but there may be times when such programs are so valuable that you will feel like borrowing the money to keep the child involved.

Clubs

On the other hand, the cost of club participation is quite minimal. Such programs as Scouts, Y-programs, or church clubs such as Awana, Brigade, Pioneer Girls, G.A., or R.A. offer children a variety of activities at a very low cost.

Although these clubs don't usually offer highly competitive games, the programs are varied enough to satisfy most interests. The meetings usually include some time for games, crafts, memory work, reading, singing, and special skills. At the same time, each of these clubs is based on the noble purpose of teaching the child some desirable virtues. Although the club may not always be successful, at least the purpose is clear; and your child will be encouraged to join into noble activities.

Another good thing about these clubs is that they offer the child as much or as little participation as he and the family want. If your child wants a casual relationship with Scouts, he can have a casual relationship. On the other hand, if he wants to throw himself into the scouting program, it can consume all of his free time. Although the immediate supervisors may not totally understand this, and they may try to make you feel guilty for less than complete involvement, the program is still there to provide you and your child with what you want and need from it. Don't be afraid to pick and choose.

Since these clubs are usually identified with a specific school or church, you won't have any trouble finding one. Which club you and your child select is a matter of interest. Although each club has a slightly different emphasis, they all begin with a noble purpose and offer an abundance of reasonable activities and services.

Obviously, your primary-age child has a wide assortment of choices for participation in outside activities. In fact, many of these organizations actively recruit, so it would be quite easy for him to develop such a schedule that he could disrupt the family activities every night of the week.

In this case, you and your child may need to learn the meaning of a new word—*no*. He just can't join everything. He has to make some choices.

It is important for both of you to remember that these outside organizations are designed to supplement the family and even school activities. When they begin to dominate the family schedule, your child is too involved.

With the proper emphasis, participation in these outside activities can be immensely educational, giving your child an opportunity to practice his new sense of independence and social skills and giving him some direction for use of his free time and talent. But I am old-fashioned enough to believe that the family responsibility is first.

Chapter 15 at a Glance

1. When your child starts school, his whole world expands, and this expanded world will include outside recreational, artistic, and social opportunities.
2. As the child gets more involved, there will be time and commitment conflicts. You need to anticipate these and arrange the family priorities beforehand.
3. Your child will have to learn to make choices, particularly if he is talented.

16

At Home Alone

Social scientists frequently invent strange names for human behavior. One of the recent additions to the list is the term *latchkey kids* which is used to designate those school-age children who either come home from school to an empty house or leave in the morning after the adults have already gone to work.

Most of the publicity the term has created has usually leaned toward the negative. Magazine and newspaper articles and radio and television reports not only give us the statistics of the huge number of children who are actually latchkey kids, but they also point out all the possible dangers involved with this activity. Since the practice is so widespread, the issue deserves some attention here, even with parents who are at home when the children get back from school.

Obviously, the topic is deeper than mere statistics and frightening warnings. First, I am not sure I am qualified to question a parent's motive for leaving a child in an empty house. You know your situations and you know your circumstances. You are the one with the responsibility of making the decisions that are most beneficial to all family members. But if you are considering a latchkey situation for your child, either before school or after school, you need to examine the possibility from at least two dimensions—safety and social relationships.

Since I am writing about first, second, and third graders, I have my greatest concern in the safety area. I suspect I have some mother-hen tendencies, but I seem to want all my chicks clustered under the safety of my wing all the time. This safety and age question keeps showing its ugly head throughout child rearing. When is he old enough to cross the street? When is he mature enough to leave without a baby-sitter? When do we buy him a bicycle and spread his energy over the whole neighborhood? When do we trust him with the car? Do we insist on curfews?

These are actually all the same questions as: Do I let him come home from school to an empty house? Is it safe?

Of course, the answer to that question depends on several factors; some you can control and some you can't. You have to consider the quality of the neighborhood, the maturity level of the child, the energy of the child, the proximity of neighbors, and your own feelings.

After you have considered all these factors, and you decide that your child is mature enough to assume responsibility for his own unsupervised care for a part of the day, you now need to take charge of those factors you can control. You need to insure that you have provided some basic elements of safety. Let me suggest some of those.

1. Teach your child to use the telephone. He is old enough to handle this whether he is going to be home alone or not. I am sure you have heard about all the proper techniques the child should use to keep from giving too much information to the wrong party. Make sure he knows not to tell anyone that he is home alone. Make sure he knows how to take a message. Make sure he knows how to guard information about himself. I am sure that you know all this and that you have told your child, but this is more than mere telling. Now is the time to teach him. Tell him how to respond, then practice with him. Let him pick up the receiver and talk to you as if you were a stranger calling the house. Make up several different stories and see how the child handles himself.

Try to get him confused or flustered. This may seem cruel while you are doing it, but this kind of role playing could pay off.

Make sure your child knows how to dial either your work phone or a nearby neighbor. Remember to have him practice this every once in a while so the number is automatic for him. If you want to go further you may want to make sure he knows the numbers of the fire department and police. Or, if you are always available at your work phone, you may choose to have these calls come to you.

2. Prepare the child's after-school snack before you leave the house.   We really have a bad combination here; I suspect everybody, teachers and students alike, needs that after-school snack, but fire is one of the biggest safety risks with children in the home. Minimize that risk by having the child's snack prepared so he won't have to turn on any cooking equipment.

3. Plan fire escape routes in your home and practice them occasionally so the whole family is always prepared.   This doesn't take long, and it can be turned into a fun family experience. We always hope we never have to use such information, but we need to practice just in case.

4. Make sure there is a neighbor close by who can help your child if he needs help.

5. Give the child some chores to do while he is waiting for you to get home.   I realize that it would be much simpler just to have him perch in front of the TV and sit there in a stupor until you get home, but those chores will help the time pass faster and will encourage the child to feel that everyone in the family has some of the family responsibility. This way, he will probably assume his role with more maturity.

6. If you have more than one child at home, make sure you have a good working relationship with the one you leave in charge. You have put a big burden of responsibility on that child. Make sure he knows he can talk with you. Make sure you know his thoughts and feelings. If he is missing some of his own childhood activities such as after-school clubs or sports to take care of other children at home, make sure you provide him with ample opportunities to make up what he has missed. Although I have seen some children mature into the responsibility of the family baby-sitter role with tons of responsibility at a very young age, those children will need some time to be children without all that responsibility. Help your leader!

From my list, you can begin to formulate your own based on your circumstances. If you are going to leave a child at home alone for part of the day, your first task is to do everything you can to provide for his safety. It still won't be as if you were there, but you can minimize the possible dangers.

This leads us to the social relationship dimension; but I am not as concerned about this as I am about the safety features. If you are a sensitive, caring parent, leaving your child at home alone for part of the day probably won't do much to alter the family situation. You can still have a solid, happy family life after you get home. There is still time for praising, hugging, reading, affirming, and all those other activities that make family life special to both children and parents.

The problem here is not the child at home alone, but it is what you do and what you value after you do get home from work. If you rush to your own chores and continue to isolate your child, then the family time is going to get out of whack. But you can control this by just making sure you understand what is most important. In fact, this is one reason why I recommend chores instead of television as a baby-sitter. Since the child has helped you accomplish some of your work, he now deserves some of your attention.

Although the research is rather sparse here, the available material tends to support me. A few years ago, a limited study indicated that children with at least one parent at home through the day got into more school problems than those with working parents. Of course, this isn't a definitive position, but it does indicate that you can make family life significant for your child even though he has to spend some time at home alone.

As a final word, let me remind you that your child needs to know how to get in touch with you at all times. Every principal has his horror stories about this. My most persuasive story is about a young man who fell and broke his arm during basketball class—a compound fracture just above the wrist. After a hurried trip to the hospital, that young man and I waited in the emergency room for three hours while the police tried to track down his mother who was on a neighborhood visiting spree. While I regaled him with every funny story I had ever heard, that brave fellow waited three hours without so much as a painkiller. That day I vowed to urge all parents to make sure the children can find them in case of an emergency.

Chapter 16 at a Glance

1. If you have to leave your child at home alone, provide for his safety.
2. Teach your child to use the phone.
3. Give the child chores to do. This will make time go faster.
4. Make family time together significant. If your work prevents you from being together as much as you would like, make the time together fruitful and pleasant. Make sure your child knows that he is more important than some of your tasks!

17
Time and Energy Trials

For the past forty Septembers, I have started to school in some capacity or another—student, teacher, principal. It really isn't a bad life, particularly if you happen to like yellow vehicles and the smell of new denim. But there is one aspect that never gets any easier—readjusting the body clock to run on the school schedule. School runs on schedule all right, whether the teachers and students are ready or not. Not only does the body have to be somewhere at a specific time, but the mind has to turn on and off according to someone else's routine.

The child in the first, second, or third grade who is adjusting to all this for the first time may not see the thrill of the challenge. You may have to help him.

For one thing, people who run schools, newspapers, or money-lending institutions seem to have an obsession with the virtue of promptness. The combination of a ringing bell and a vacant seat seems to disturb most teachers, and when one is disturbed, a minute is only briefly shorter than eternity. That minute may not seem like much when the child stops to pick a flower or chase a bee or pet a dog; but to the people in charge of the school, that minute is a major issue. (Incidentally, in my list of compulsive timers, I forgot to mention bus drivers. They bow to Greenwich precision, too.) If your child is ever going to please enough people to be successful in school, you will need to help him understand this demand to be there when he is supposed to be.

You can begin this emphasis by timing the journey to school

before the term begins and he makes everybody angry by being a minute late. Walk the route with the child. And if he is the kind of person who takes little curious side trips, allow a few extra minutes for such emergencies as a new dog on the block or roses in bloom. But get him out the door in time for him to make the journey. That way, if the principal's secretary calls you to yell about his being late two days in a row, you can act surprised and arrogantly competent by saying, "I don't understand that at all. We have timed the route. I *know* how long it should take him to get there. He leaves the house on time. Are you sure he is not dallying on the playground?" That ought to put her on the defensive.

Seriously though, starting your child to school on time may require making some adjustments throughout the day. For one thing, you and the child will have to get up early enough to allow time for dressing emergencies, such as a button popping off or the shoes being left in the sandbox overnight. And you need to allow enough time for him to have a good breakfast. That is enough of that sermon. You have heard it all before; but every primary teacher I have ever met assures me that by nine-thirty she can pick out the children who have had a good breakfast.

If all this preschool activity demands that you or the child get up a little earlier, you will have to compensate by going to bed a little earlier. And this routine doesn't just happen with some psychological event called "Labor Day." You have to start a few weeks earlier preparing for it. I realize that it is tough to put an active six-year-old to bed while the August sun is still shining, but you can gradually lead into an earlier bedtime by planning some restful activities for the end of the day. Put the child in his room with books or drawing or counting. His body should get the message to rest.

Another problem I have is that every summer I get into the habit of taking a little afternoon nap. But the people who run the schools frown on such things. So every September I find myself going through withdrawal trauma. I find myself fighting off sleep at a time when someone is expecting my mind to be active and alert. So if your child is in the habit of an afternoon nap, you may want to help him gradually break into the routine of staying awake all day and going to sleep a little earlier in the evening.

If you suspect that your child is going to have difficulty resetting his body clock to the school schedule, it will help you to know what the school schedule is. Talk to the teacher and find out what is expected of the child at specific times during the day. Usually, primary teachers begin the day with either math or reading, depending on what the teacher thinks is most important. Obviously, these teachers feel that the early part of the morning is the choicest teaching time of the day. Of course, the total school schedule will dictate some of the routine. For example, if the first graders leave the classroom to go to P.E. they will go when the instructor and facilities are available, even though this may not be the most desirable time of the day. You and your child will just have to understand the total school demands.

While we are on the subject of body schedules, do the teacher a favor and go light on the sugar at lunchtime. An overdose of sugar can pump a lot of children into a state of immediate irrational energy at a time when the teacher is expecting them to sit silently while she reads an interesting book to the class. If your child comes home for lunch, you can control this with a balanced meal. However, if he takes his lunch, you may want to pack an orange instead of the Ding Dong. Since you don't know whether he is going to touch that peanut butter sandwich, you can at least prevent the possibility of his eating only sugar.

School also introduces the child to a new concept of body rhythms—the division of energies. There is physical energy and mental energy—physical exercise and mental exercise. When either of the energies is all spent, we are exhausted; but we might not always recognize why we are exhausted so we don't know how to rest.

In normal situations, preschool children simply have more freedom of physical movement than they will have after they start school. Most children come equipped with a natural buzzer. They know when they have sat too long or have concentrated too long on some nonphysical project; so when they have the opportunity, they will get up and move around until they balance out the physical and mental energy levels.

But in the classroom, the child usually doesn't have the physical freedom to make that adjustment. Since schoolwork is predominantly mental, he spends his mental energy without sufficient physical breaks to keep the system in balance. Although the scheduled P.E. classes help, they simply aren't frequent enough to keep the child from becoming mentally exhausted. Most experts advise college-age students—I repeat, college-age students—to keep their study minds alert by relaxing and exercising ten minutes out of every hour. No wonder the six-year-old wears out from the routines of first-grade learning.

When the child becomes mentally exhausted, he needs exercise, not inactivity. Some children know that naturally, and they will get their physical exercise. Oh, how they get their physical exercise. If your child is one of those who won't be cheated out of his physical movement, you may be a little shocked by his after-school behavior. You may find yourself asking such questions as: "What happened to my little lamb? He has always been so docile and quiet. Where is he learning all this stuff? Is school teaching him to be bad?" If you get a rather abrupt change in behavior after your child starts school, you may want to check with the teacher just to make sure; but don't be surprised to find that this is just a natural reaction to his being mentally active and physically dormant for the past six hours.

Some children simply have more difficulty adjusting their

bodies to the physical inactivity of school. If your child is having this problem, you may want to check with your family doctor. A few children do have a condition called hyperactivity. In this case, the doctors usually prescribe a stimulant which slows the child down. But true hyperactivity is rare and can be difficult to diagnose. Don't accept just one opinion.

There is a difference between an active child and a hyperactive child, but that difference may not be immediately obvious during the last period of the school day.

On the other hand, your child may react to his exhausting day by coming home, wolfing down the snack, and stretching out on the floor for six hours of passive television staring.

Both children need the same therapy. They need controlled physical involvement and activity. You can either appoint yourself the family recreation director in charge of such things as walking, jogging, raking, biking, or building. Or you may want to seek help from one of those outside activities we talked about in chapter 15.

If your child is as slow to adjusting to new situations as I am, he is going to need some help resetting his body clock to the school schedule. And this isn't just a once-in-a-lifetime event. He will have to go through it year after year. With love and common sense and commonsense love, you can help him make it. So now let's devote our attention to a study of commonsense love.

Chapter 17 at a Glance

1. One of the most difficult adjustments to school life is resetting the body clock to follow the school schedule.

2. Anticipate this problem. Start early. Help the child make the adjustment before school starts.

3. Expect some unused physical energy when the child gets home from school.

4. If your child has a serious problem of controlling his physical movement, he may have a medical problem. Consult a physician.

5. Hyperactivity is actually a rare condition. If someone suggests your child has it, check with several experts before you make a definite decision.

18

Commonsense Love

I know you love your child. You have loved him ever since he was born, and this is a constant love. Regardless of what he does or becomes, your love will stay unchanged. This is something he can always count on. But when your child starts school, both of you will encounter some circumstances that will give you new opportunities to express that love in practical terms. For one thing, you will find that you will need a responsive love in reacting to situations rather than creating them. Let me try to clarify that. When your child is at home with you all day, you create learning situations. You develop the scenes and control the variables. But when your child starts school, he is going to encounter social situations and learning situations that create special kinds of problems for him.

Since you didn't establish these, they are outside your control. Now, you have to use commonsense love in reacting to a situation where you are something of an outsider. You can share vicariously with your child in what he is going through, but you simply don't have the same emotional involvement as you would have had if you had created the situation.

For example, during his school career, your child is going to experience success, but he is also going to experience failure. As a parent, I am a lot better at helping my children though successes than helping them through failures; and if I were arranging things, I would provide situations where they did more succeeding than failing. Unfortunately, or perhaps fortunately, the people outside the home aren't as sensitive as I am; so as the child enters that broader world, I am going to have to learn how to react to his failures; and I am going to have to teach him how to manage. In other words, I am going to have to put love to the practical test.

When your child first wanders away from the nest and treks off to school, there are a whole bundle of setbacks and frustrations waiting to snare him. He isn't learning something as quickly as his classmates. He lost the race at recess. The class bully is pushing him around. His artwork was not selected for the bulletin board. His crayon broke. The teacher yelled at him for running to the window to watch the fire truck. Two other kids always sit in the same seat on the bus and won't let him in. In the P.E. bombardment game he was the last one chosen. Some kids teased him when he got glasses, or braces, or a black eye.

With all the trouble in the Mideast, these may not sound like major problems, but when a person is only seven years old and his world doesn't even include a Mideast, these are real frustrations. The people who would help him through these trying times need to understand the significance of such problems. They are real problems and they need attention.

How you respond to these real problems depends largely on what kind of person you are and what kind of person your child is. You may want to try diversion. If the child is suffering some setbacks at school, help get his mind off these problems by creating some successful learning experiences outside school. Have him wash the car. Teach him to ride a bike without training wheels. Open a savings account. Take him to a movie. It could be that school has introduced him to the first real setback he has ever experienced, and this could be devastating to his confidence. By your establishing diversionary situations where he can succeed, he may regain his confidence sufficiently that he can even work out his own frustrations at school.

On the other hand, you may want to try direct instruction. As your child encounters these new learning experiences, such as bullies or rude children (or even rude adults), you may want to give him some specific directions on how to manage relationships with those people who would take advantage. If you decide to go this route, make sure your directions are workable. Too often we give instructions that are easier to give than to follow. If you sense that your child is frightened of the class bully, try not to tell him to punch the guy in the nose. Regardless of what you think of the role of violence in human relationships, that is poor advice. Would you punch Mr. T in the nose? If you choose to give instructions to help your child handle setbacks, you need to be very specific. Make sure he understands how he can implement the information you have provided. If you give directions from Scripture, make sure he sees the practical application.

A third technique for dealing with your child's setbacks and failures is consistency. Regardless of the kinds of problems he brings home from school and regardless of the kinds of problems he creates himself, maintain a constant, consistent, loving environment just so he can have the experience of being comfortable and accepted for at least part of his day. This consistency and acceptance will provide him with the opportunity to refuel his confidence and identity so he can face the more unpleasant situations.

This leads us to another point. During the period when your child is adjusting to school life, he may actually create an unusual trap for himself. When school first starts, he will probably discover a new wave of independence; and he may choose to flaunt that a bit. Now that he has friends and a life of his own, he simply doesn't need family support as much as he once did. He may try to draw away by building some fences to show you that he is growing. But when the trials, frustrations, setbacks, and failures come, he may want to find solace by returning to a simpler, safer time. That is a fairly normal reaction. When the present gets me down, I find some comfort in remembering the safety of the past.

But if your child has already built the fences, he may not know how to get back to a time when it was all right to sit on your lap and earn your hugs. Since he now has the power to read himself, he may not know how to return to a time when you read the bedtime story and tucked him in. This is why I recommend consistency. Regardless of how independent he tries to become, make sure you are giving enough cues that he knows he is still welcome to retreat to your lap and regroup.

Close, unthreatening human contact is good therapy for just about anybody, and it is particularly important for this child who is still more child than adult, regardless of his adventures into the real world. And this is not just a situation confined to first grade. It is quite possible that your child can make it through the first grade and perhaps even the second grade before he encounters any significant frustrations. During this whole process when he is growing, when he is likely to meet problems that demand your commonsense reaction, keep the door open and the lap welcome in case he needs a bit of reassurance which comes only through a real demonstration of love and approval.

Chapter 18 at a Glance

1. Keep your love and affection consistent even though your child may indicate he has grown beyond such things. He may need to retreat occasionally in the face of school problems.

2. Consider his problems as real problems. Although we know that he will live through such things as being the last one chosen at recess, he still needs understanding.
3. Make sure your child has some successes to balance his failures. If he isn't meeting successes, engineer some for him.

19

Love and Approval

My wise professor used to say, "Having a child is taking out a twenty-year mortgage on your emotions, energy, time, and money." As my children were growing, I decided he knew what he was talking about. Now that my children are grown, I have decided that the mortgage is even longer than he said.

Throughout this book, I have focused discussion on helping children at a very special age—the age between six and eight when they first discover the world beyond home and parents In asking for your understanding, I have described some emotional, physical, and educational situations which people this age usually encounter; and I have made some specific suggestions which I hope help you help your child during this time of adjustment. But the most significant piece of advice I have to give is the counsel of my professor. Remember the length of the mortgage.

In the normal process, people grow from infancy into childhood, from childhood into adolescence, and from adolescence into adulthood. You don't want to cheat your child out of an opportunity to make the most of childhood since this is the only one he will ever have; at the same time you do a disservice to your child and to yourself to rivet your attention too tightly to a fixed moment in the growth process. Every decision you make, every action you take, every word and every hug have two consequences—the immediate and the long range. You need to make sure you see those two blended together because the other people in your child's life at this stage may be limited to focusing on only one.

For example, teachers, by the very nature of their assignments, tend to see immediate actions and results. All the influence that a specific teacher will ever have in the life of your child must be packed into nine months. She has to see the results of her work in that same limited school year. Sometimes this restriction to the immediate intensifies the teacher's response to growth or lack of growth in a specific area.

One of my young friends started to kindergarten this year. Since he and I are pals, we have had frequent conversations about such things as sports, movies, ice cream trucks, books, and God. I find him a stimulating conversationalist. He is polite, and he is confident enough to be at ease around adults. After his third day in school, he came trudging home with a note attached to his shirt:

Dear Mr. and Mrs. X:
   Because of his disregard and disinterest for school and class-room policy, George's behavior has become a matter of immedi-ate concern. Please call and make an appointment to meet with me.

Sincerely,
Mrs. Kindergarten Teacher

I think I know why parents are often frightened of their chil-dren's teachers. I would be trembling too if I had to meet that lady. But after I got those parents quieted down and reassured of some self-dignity, I persuaded them to muster the courage to go see her. It seems that George did not know how to write his name as well as the other children, so he turned in his papers without a name. Personally, I thought that was a rather intelligent solution to the problem, but turning in a paper without a name is an abso-lute no-no in the academic world. I think the teacher was also disturbed because George didn't show any noticeable remorse over his inability to perform. He had simply not learned the right attitude toward his weakness.

I am probably coming down too hard on this teacher, but she does illustrate my point. She was simply too limited to immediate consequences. She couldn't see the long range. George is all right. He is capable, active, and happy. If nothing more traumatic than this happens to him, he is going to have a full childhood and a solid life. I hope his parents saved that note. In fifteen years, when George comes home from college, he and his parents should have a chuckle remembering the incident.

So this is your challenge as you help your child get acclimated to school and school activities: You need to respond to the joys and frustrations of the moment, but you also need to keep your responses in the perspective of a total life.

To help you keep that perspective, remember that your child is unique. If you have more than one child, you have already discovered that. Each is different with different emotions, different responses, and different needs. During the past twenty-five years as a teacher, I have seen more than three thousand children, and I assure you that each is unique. In His infinite wisdom, the Creator chose not to make any two alike. Since your child is unique, he deserves a unique relationship with you. Read the advice books, listen to the speeches, study the research reports; but remember all the time that this special child is unique. If he doesn't fit into one of the charts, you don't need to panic. The Creator who made him unique also promised you the wisdom you need to respond to his unique personality. Your child may grow according to schedule, but he may not. He may learn in an acceptable pattern, or he may not. In the midst of his becoming conformed to the patterns of culture—discipline, order, decoding—he will still be at war with himself to maintain his uniqueness. Help him in the battle.

But that is a big and sneaky piece of advice. To be able to lend support in his both becoming educated and staying unique, you will need to know your child. You will need to know how he is like other children and how he is different. You will need to know when he is on a natural schedule and when he is just being lazy.

In order to know that, you will have to spend a lot of time with him, gathering the data and showing your love. And if you spend enough time with your child to know him that well, he will most likely respond to the attention and have a happy, successful primary career, despite your proficiency with all the techniques I have suggested.

And both of you will have gained. Time remembered is never as long as time lived, and at best, one's primary career is only a fleeting moment in the space of a lifetime. There is so much packed into such a few weeks, so many new beginnings. Between the ages of six and eight, the chattel of your mortgage will start to school for the first and only time in his life. He will learn to read for the first and only time. He will have first-, second-, and third-grade teachers for the first and only time. He will memorize his arithmetic facts, write his name, and perform a variety of new skills and acquire a variety of new attitudes.

As he grows past this stage of life and enters other eras, let's pray that he leaves with more than mere skills and attitudes. Let's pray that during that time of "first and only" he has picked up some events, some significant moments which constitute the stuff of memories, happy memories resting at the threshold of his mind—moments to be called back into the memory to fill those empty mental spaces as he waits at a red light or just before he drops off to sleep at night, or when he helps your grandchild learn to count past twenty.

As you help him master the skill required to function in his changing world, you can also help him drive the pegs on which to hang those memories. Soon, too soon, his primary years will be over only to live in memory; but if the two of you share his primary years together, you will always hold the memories together. And that is the bond of parenthood.

Chapter 19 at a Glance

1. Child rearing is a matter of perspective. What does it mean now? What will this mean next week? What will this mean twenty years from now?
2. That is the test.